CHRIST PREEMINENT

Studies in Philippians

by Theodore H. Epp

Director
Back to the Bible Broadcast

A
BACK TO THE BIBLE
PUBLICATION

D0097314

Back to the Bible

Lincoln, Nebraska 68501

5000 printed to date—1980
(5-8900—5M—10)
ISBN 0-8474-1294-6

Unless otherwise identified, all Scripture quotations are
from the New American Standard Bible.

Cover Photo by Bill Myers.

Printed in the United States of America

Foreword

When Theodore Epp first began meditating and studying for a series of radio messages on the Book of Philippians, his heart was especially burdened that people would do "right thinking about God." He had observed much confused thinking about who Jesus Christ is and what He wants to do in the believer's life.

Mr. Epp realized the Book of Philippians would serve as a corrective to wrong thinking in these areas. He also knew the book would minister spiritually to believers who have no special problems but who have a sincere desire to know Christ better.

This series was first presented over the international radio network of the Back to the Bible Broadcast. The messages are now placed into book form so they can have an even wider ministry.

It was a privilege to have a part in preparing these messages for publication. As I worked through the messages Mr. Epp had already given on radio, it was like a personal revival to carefully consider Jesus Christ as He is presented in the Book of Philippians.

—Harold J. Berry, Instructor
Grace College of the Bible
Omaha, Nebraska

Contents

Chapter 1

Christ Preeminent

The Book of Philippians is exceedingly rich in spiritual truths. In order to gain the most from a study of this book, it is necessary to know some of the historical background as well as to have an overview of the entire book.

The Book of Philippians does not divide easily into separate parts as do some other books of the Bible, such as Romans. For instance, the first two and a half chapters of Romans emphasize the lost state of mankind. The next two and a half tell of God's wonderful plan of salvation. The next three tell how to live the Christian life by overcoming sin through the power of the Spirit. The next three deal with the past, present and future of the nation of Israel. And the last four chapters of Romans form a practical application based on what had been said up to that point.

The Book of Philippians is not as easily divided. Although the book has only four chapters, the statements in those four chapters are so interwoven that it is impossible to neatly divide them into sections.

Romans and Philippians Contrasted

Note some interesting contrasts between Romans and Philippians. Romans is filled with doctrine and technique for Christian living whereas Philippians reveals those doctrines and techniques being put to the test in life and action. Romans speaks more to the mind, or intellect, by presenting doctrines that every believer needs to know. Philippians speaks more to the heart, or the emotions and will, because it emphasizes how a person should respond to the facts. Romans emphasizes knowing the facts whereas Philippians emphasizes knowing a Person—Jesus Christ.

This is not to say that one book is more important than another; rather, it emphasizes that each makes its own special contribution to the written Word of God. The more we know about the doctrines in the Book of Romans, the more we will have a keener appreciation of what is said in Philippians, where we see these doctrines translated into daily, living experiences.

Mankind today seems to be knowledgeable about everything except God. Even the scientific world is continually searching for the origin of the universe. This curiosity has been the basis for many explorations in this world as well as in outer space. One does not have to go to the moon, however, to discover how this world came into existence; one only needs to go to the Word of God. Genesis 1:1 clearly states: "In the beginning God created the heavens and the earth." John 1:1-4 says, "In the beginning was the Word, and the Word was with God, and the Word was God. He was in the beginning with God. All things came into being through Him; and apart from Him nothing came into being that has come into being. In Him was life; and the life was the light of men."

Because mankind wants to continue in darkness, people search and search for explanations and do not come to the source of truth, the Word of God.

We approach the Book of Philippians with the assumption that we are studying the actual Word of God as it was given to the Apostle Paul and that in the original writing it was without error because it was inspired by God Himself.

Background Information

Whenever one is studying one of the New Testament epistles, or letters, it is helpful if he can learn background information about the particular church or people involved. Because Paul's letters grew out of his missionary travels, one can usually find something in the Book of the Acts where Paul's missionary journeys are described that gives background for the letters he wrote. This is true concerning Philippians.

Paul's Call to Macedonia

Acts 16 records Paul's experiences as he founded the church at Philippi. During Paul's second missionary journey, he was traveling through Asia Minor (modern Turkey), visiting the churches he had established on his first missionary journey. At Troas, Paul had a vision of a man from Macedonia (modern Greece) urging him to come to Macedonia (Acts 16:9). The Book of the Acts records: "And when he had seen the vision, immediately we sought to go into Macedonia, concluding that God had called us to preach the gospel to them. Therefore putting out to sea from Troas, we ran a straight course to Samothrace, and on the day following to Neapolis; and from there to Philippi, which is a leading city of the district of Macedonia, a Roman colony; and we were staying in this city for some days" (vv. 10-12).

It is evident from Acts 16 that God was distinctly leading Paul and those who were with him. Luke, the author of the Book of the Acts, was in the group, too, and that is why verse 10 says, "We sought to go into Macedonia."

The first contact that Paul and his companions had in Macedonia was with some women. As Paul preached the gospel, the Lord opened the heart of Lydia to respond to what he had said (v. 14). She became the first convert in Europe. Not only was she saved, so was her entire household (v. 15).

Paul and Silas in Prison

This was a very positive result from their first contact, but things soon took a turn in the opposite direction. Paul cast a demon out of a woman who was bringing her masters much profit through fortune-telling (Acts 16:16-18). Her masters were so upset that they turned the people and the authorities of the city against Paul and Silas, and as a result, Paul and Silas were beaten and thrown into the prison.

Think of it! Paul and Silas had been faithful in preaching the gospel, but they were thrown into prison because of it. They were put in the security ward of the inner prison, and their feet were placed in stocks. They could not lie down because their lacerated backs would have been too sore, so all they could do was sit up. But instead of feeling sorry for themselves, they prayed and sang praises to God.

The jailer had been sleeping on duty, but he was awakened by the earthquake. When he saw the doors of the prison standing open, he immediately assumed the prioners had escaped. Knowing that his life would have to be given for theirs because he allowed them to escape, the jailer drew his sword and was about to commit suicide. As soon as he saw what was about to happen, Paul cried out, "Do yourself no harm, for we are all here!" (v. 28).

After the jailer had entered the prison and found all the prisoners still there, he came under such conviction that he asked, "Sirs, what must I do to be saved?" (v. 30). Paul and Silas responded, "Believe in the Lord Jesus, and you shall be saved, you and your household" (v. 31). Although those are the only recorded words of Paul and Silas, the next verse adds, "They spoke the word of the Lord to him together with all who were in his house" (v. 32). So the Word of God was given to the jailer and his household so they knew precisely where to place their faith.

How interesting to notice that the church in Philippi really began in a prison. This was God's way of reaching the jailer, who otherwise might never have been brought under conviction. And how important it was also that Paul and Silas were living victoriously even though circumstances had gone against them. They were not wallowing in self-pity in the prison; rather, they were praying and singing hymns of praise to God (v. 25).

Salvation of Households

Notice that not only was the jailer reached with the gospel, so was his household. This had also occurred when Lydia believed in Jesus Christ, for both she and "her household" (Acts 16:15) were baptized. The jailer and his household heard the Word of God and were baptized that same night (vv. 32,33).

There is a sense in which the Bible teaches household salvation, but this sense has been misunderstood by some. It is not that their households were automatically saved because Lydia believed and the jailer believed. One person's faith in Christ never saves another person—each individual must realize he is a sinner and personally trust Christ for his own salvation. But when one person comes to know Jesus Christ as Saviour, he can, in a sense, claim by faith the salvation of the other members of his household. Although his faith alone does not save the other members of the family, God often honors that faith by using that individual to reach the other members of his household. So while one person's faith cannot save other people, the one person can believe that God will bring the others to salvation.

The emphasis on one's household is seen even back in Exodus 12, which records the events that took place when the Israelites were preparing to flee the land of Egypt. God told Moses and Aaron: "Speak to all the congregation of Israel, saying, 'On the tenth of this month they are each one to take a lamb for themselves, according to their fathers' households, a lamb for each household' " (v. 3). So even at the time of the exodus the emphasis was not just on each individual but on each household.

In the case of the Philippian jailer, the same night that he and his household believed in Jesus Christ, they were all baptized (Acts 16:33). The jailer washed the wounds of Paul and Silas and gave them a meal. The Scripture notes that the jailer "rejoiced greatly, having believed in God with his whole household" (v. 34).

Paul and Silas Leave Philippi

When daybreak came, the leaders of the city sent word to the jailer to release Paul and Silas. However, Paul refused to go. Paul said, "They have beaten us in public without trial, men who are Romans, and have thrown us into prison; and now are they sending us away secretly? No indeed! But let them come themselves and bring us out" (Acts 16:37).

When word was taken back to the city leaders that Paul and Silas were Roman citizens, the leaders became very concerned because they knew that no Roman citizen should be beaten without a trial. This meant the leaders could be in trouble with the Roman government, so they came to Paul and Silas and "kept begging them to leave the city" (v. 39). Instead of doing this immediately, however, Paul and Silas "went out of the prison and entered the house of Lydia, and when they saw the brethren, they encouraged them and departed" (v. 40). Paul refused to leave the city immediately just so the leaders could save face; he first met with fellow believers to encourage them and then left the city at his own convenience.

In a sense, the church at Philippi started in a prison, and ten years later Paul was writing from prison to the Philippians to encourage them to always rejoice in everything. In fact, forms of the word "rejoice" occur 12 times in Paul's letter to the Philippians. It is interesting that Paul's ministry to the Philippians was so directly connected with prisons—first, a prison in Philippi where the jailer and his household were won to Christ and, ten years later, a prison in Rome from which he wrote to encourage the Philippians.

Prominence of Women

Also as background to the Book of Philippians, consider the place of prominence held by the women. It was the women who met by the riverside to pray (Acts 16:13), and their prayers were probably the basis of the Macedonian call Paul received to come to their area to preach the gospel (v. 9). Eternity will someday reveal the trophies which have been won down through the centuries by the faithful prayers of women.

The Scriptures specifically mention many other women. Consider Ruth of Moab who placed her faith in God and became an ancestor of David, which placed her in the ancestral line of the Lord Jesus Christ.

Hannah prayed to God for a son and was given Samuel in response to her request. Esther, a Jewish slave girl in a foreign land, became queen and was used of God to deliver the Israelites. Elizabeth, although not much information is given about her, figured prominently as the mother of John the Baptist.

Consider also the virgin Mary, the mother of Jesus. She was not sinless, as some teach, but she gave birth to the sinless Son of God, who was conceived in her by the Holy Spirit. It was a high privilege to be chosen as the mother of the Son of God and then to serve Him in so many ways as He grew to maturity.

We have already referred to Lydia, who was a businesswoman from Thyatira. She and her household were the first converts in Europe as well as the first believers in Philippi.

There was also the young woman out of whom Paul cast a demon, which resulted in the imprisonment of Paul and Silas.

Notice the words the demon-possessed girl spoke: "These men are bond-servants of the Most High God, who are proclaiming to you the way of salvation" (Acts 16:17).

Considering women in relation to the church of Philippi, two are specifically mentioned by name in Philippians 4, Euodia and Syntyche, and we will discuss them more completely as we come to that chapter.

Theme of Philippians

There are several important considerations to be made concerning the theme of the Book of Philippians. Before beginning a detailed study of any book, it is good to get an overview of it in order to establish a main theme the writer had in mind.

Before restating the main theme of Paul's letter to the Philippians, let us underscore what the theme is *not*. The main theme is not doctrine, for it is evident that Paul was not writing to the Philippians to communicate the doctrinal beliefs of Christianity. Neither is the main theme of the book that of error, for there are only minor warnings in the book that would indicate Paul was concerned about error. Nor is the main theme the ungodly living of the Philippians, for the letter does not dwell on that subject; in fact, the word "sin" is not once mentioned in Paul's letter to the Philippians.

Having considered what the main theme is not, let us consider what it is. Philippians was a very personal letter from Paul to the Philippian believers, presenting the essential elements of vital Christian living. Although there are different opinions as to the main theme of Philippians, from my study of the letter I think the best theme that could be selected is "Christian Experience." Paul was writing to the Philippians to let them know what should be the experience of the believer as he is in union with his Lord and Saviour, Jesus Christ, regardless of the circumstances he may be experiencing.

Other interpreters of the Book of Philippians have emphasized the aspect of joy which Paul wrote much about. In fact, because the words "joy" and "rejoice" occur 12 times in the four chapters, some have called it "The Book of Joy." Others have emphasized what Paul had to say concerning the believer's having the mind of Christ. Since the word "mind" occurs 12 times, they feel the theme has to do with what our attitudes should be.

However, the more I study the Book of Philippians, the more I am convinced that Paul was writing to the Philippians to emphasize that Christ is the divine source, the constant center, the total outworking and the strength—or power—for a consistent Christian life. The prominence given to the Lord Jesus Christ in the Book of Philippians is indicated by the fact that reference to Him by nouns and pronouns is made at least 70 times in the 104 verses.

The Christian's experience, or daily walk, is a matter of his relationship to Jesus Christ. This is what we will see throughout the Book of Philippians. Colossians 3:11 states the truth in this way: "Christ is all, and in all."

The four chapters of Philippians reveal four different movements in the main theme of Christian experience. Of course, all Christian experience centers in the Person of Christ, so in a sense Jesus Christ Himself is the theme, whereas a characteristic such as joy is the fruit of living in Jesus Christ, which is true Christian experience.

Key Verses in Philippians

The key verse in each chapter expresses the main emphasis of that entire chapter.

Christ, the Believer's Life

The key verse of Philippians 1 is verse 21: "For to me to live is Christ" (KJV). Everything in this chapter centers on the thought that Christ is the believer's life and experience. He is the source of it, the beginning of it and the strength of it—He is everything concerning the believer's life. The Christian's life is not a mere system of ethics. The Christian's life is Jesus Christ, and a certain code of ethics results from that life. The life itself is that which flows from Christ. It finds its righteousness, or rightness, in Christ. Whatever a Christian does results from the relationship he has with Christ, so in this sense the doing comes from the being. That Christ is the source and the power for performing all of the Christian life is seen from verse 6: "Being confident of this very thing, that he which hath begun a good work in you will perform it until the day of Jesus Christ."

Christ, the Believer's Mind

Verse 5 is the key verse of Philippians 2: "Let this mind be in you, which was also in Christ Jesus" (KJV). Particularly notice the word "let." Why is it stated like this? Because Christ is already in the believer's life, as we will see in this second chapter. So we are to cooperate with Him in letting Him express Himself through us. So the main emphasis of Chapter 2 is the thought that Christ is the believer's mind.

The word "mind" occurs 12 times in the King James Version. The Greek word Paul used for mind was a word which stressed the thinking process. One who thinks in a certain way is one who is spoken of as having a certain type of mind. The believer is to think in the same way as Christ; he is to have the same kind of mind as Jesus Christ has.

Inasmuch as even today Jesus Christ indwells every believer, the Christian is to let Christ operate his mind too. Every believer is to be responsive to the mind of God. Of course, this means that a person must be born again, for only by realizing one's sinfulness and believing in Jesus Christ as his personal Saviour can one come into right relationship with Christ. When one becomes born again and is indwelt by Christ, he has the mind of Christ. So by thinking with God it is possible for him to act in harmony with God.

The beginning of Chapter 2 especially emphasizes the mind. "Being of one accord, of one mind" (v. 2, KJV). "In lowliness of mind let each esteem other better than themselves" (v. 3, KJV). "Let this mind be in you, which was also in Christ Jesus" (v. 5, KJV). By thinking with God we will act in harmony with God, and by so doing we will be acting in harmony with each other.

The mind is also emphasized in Romans 12:2: "Do not be conformed to this world, but be transformed by the renewing of your mind, that you may prove what the will of God is, that which is good and acceptable and perfect." Only as we are transformed by the renewing of the mind will we ever prove what is the good, acceptable and perfect will of God. This is the grip that God needs and wants to get on each one of us. We cannot get into the stream of God's will or God's purpose and reflect His likeness until our minds have become the willing channel of His thought life. We are to let Him think and work through us.

Christ, the Believer's Goal

The key verse in Philippians 3 is verse 10: "That I may know him, and the power of his resurrection, and the fellowship of his sufferings, being made conformable unto his death" (KJV). The key thought of this verse is "that I may know him." The central truth here is that Christ is the believer's goal.

Christ Himself is the supreme object of the believer's desire, the true goal of the believer's whole life and being. This is also seen from Romans 8:28,29. Verse 28 is familiar to most everyone: "We know that God causes all things to work together for good to those who love God, to those who are called according to His purpose." However, few seem to realize that the goal for all things working together for good is stated in the following verse: "For whom He foreknew, He also predestined to become conformed to the image of His Son." So we see even in this passage that God wants us to become like Jesus Christ. The focal point of our Christian life is Christ. When Christ was on earth, He was an example to us of glorifying the Father. Now He indwells us to enable us to do this. When Jesus was on earth, He prayed to His Heavenly Father and said, "I glorified Thee on the earth, having accomplished the work which Thou hast given Me to do" (John 17:4).

Christ, the Believer's Strength

The key verse of Philippians 4 is verse 13: "I can do all things through Christ which strengtheneth me" (KJV). This verse reveals the enabling power of Christ. The truth that is expressed in this verse is that Christ is the believer's strength.

In summary, remember that the main theme of Philippians is Christ in Christian experience and that the four chapters reveal progression of thought. Chapter 1 reveals that Christ is our life, Chapter 2 that Christ is our mind, Chapter 3 that Christ is our goal and Chapter 4 that Christ is our strength.

The progression seen in Philippians is much like that which

is seen in Colossians 2:6-10. First, there is the initial statement: "As you therefore have received Christ Jesus the Lord, so walk in him." Notice particularly the comparison indicated by the words "as" and "so." It was by faith that each individual trusted Jesus Christ as Saviour, so it is by faith that we are to live, or walk, in Him.

Then the passage goes on to state: "Having been firmly rooted and now being built up in Him and established in your faith, just as you were instructed and overflowing with gratitude" (v. 7). As Paul progressed on to encourage the Colossians to become firmly established in their faith, he then issued a warning: "See to it that no one takes you captive through philosophy and empty deception, according to the tradition of man, according to the elementary principles of the world, rather than according to Christ. For in Him all the fulness of Deity dwells in bodily form, and in Him you have been made complete, and He is the head over all rule and authority" (vv. 8-10). This passage also clearly emphasizes that everything is in Christ, and we are complete in Him.

In the four chapters of Philippians it is important to notice the progression from Chapter 1 through Chapter 4. If Christ is truly our life (ch. 1), then this life will express itself in and through our mental activity (ch. 2). The proper mental attitude of Chapter 2 leads to the supreme goal, or desire, which is Jesus Christ. The believer's desire is to be like Christ and to really know Him and thereby to go on to maturity (ch. 3). This then leads to the one and only ultimate source of strength (ch. 4). Thus, the circle leads back to Christ, our very life.

Rejoicing

Throughout the Epistle to the Philippians there is a dominant note, and that is rejoicing! It is for this reason that the Book of Philippians is often referred to as "The Epistle of Joy." Although I have chosen another theme for the letter, I agree that the element of joy, or rejoicing, is a very dominant one in the epistle. There is a command to rejoice: "Rejoice in the Lord alway: and again I say, Rejoice" (4:4, KJV). But in a sense, the rejoicing is also simply a working out of the salvation that has been worked into every believer who has trusted Christ as Saviour (see 2:12). We will comment more on this verse when we come to that portion of the epistle.

In a distinct sense, joy is really the overflow of the heart that knows Christ as its life, its mind, its goal and its strength. Only when a believer knows these aspects concerning Christ does he have full joy.

It is important to note the distinction between the words "joy" and "happiness." Happiness depends on that which happens, whereas joy in the Christian life is the result of a relationship, even though the happenings may not be pleasant in themselves.

The Example of Paul

The Apostle Paul serves as a good example to illustrate the distinctions between joy and happiness. When Paul wrote to the Philippians, it had been about ten years since he had first visited them and had been thrown into prison. Many things had happened to him during those ten years—things that would have produced anything but happiness, as one judges happiness from a human viewpoint. Some of the things that Paul endured are enumerated in his second letter to the Corinthians. Some people opposed Paul as an apostle, and the Corinthians were being confused by the controversy. Thus, Paul chose to tell the Corinthians of many things he had endured for the cause of Christ.

Paul wrote: "Are they servants of Christ? (I speak as if insane) I more so; in far more labors, in far more imprisonments, beaten times without number, often in danger of death. Five times I received from the Jews thirty-nine lashes. Three times I was beaten with rods, once I was stoned, three times I was shipwrecked, a night and a day I have spent in the deep. I have been on frequent journeys, in dangers from rivers, dangers from robbers, dangers from my countrymen, dangers from the Gentiles, dangers in the city, dangers in the wilderness, dangers on the sea, dangers among false brethren; I have been in labor and hardship, through many sleepless nights, in hunger and thirst, often without food, in cold and exposure. Apart from such external things, there is the daily pressure upon me of concern for all the churches" (II Cor. 11:23-28).

What an insight this passage gives us into the life of Paul! These were the kinds of experiences Paul had during the ten years between the time the church at Philippi was founded and the time he wrote his letter to the Philippians. There had not been many happenings that could have produced happiness, but because of his relationship with Christ he had a deep-seated joy. What Paul had endured were experiences in the physical body, but he relied on his relationship to the Lord in the midst of every circumstance. In this we find a divine paradox: That which means sorrow and suffering from a human viewpoint is viewed as joy and peace when one considers his relationship in Christ. What a tremendous God we have!

The Example of Christ

Although the Lord Jesus Christ is our supreme example in everything, this is especially true concerning peace and joy. Even when He was confronted by Satan and the cross of crucifixion, Christ spoke of peace. Just prior to going to the cross, Jesus told His disciples: "Peace I leave with you; My peace I give to you; not as the world gives, do I give to you. Let not your heart be troubled, nor let it be fearful" (John 14:27). Jesus wants to give us this same peace, and if we have trusted Him as Saviour, He dwells in us to give us His peace.

Later, Jesus told His disciples, "These things I have spoken to you, that in Me you may have peace. In the world you have tribulation, but take courage; I have overcome the world" (16:33).

Although these references refer to peace, Jesus specifically referred also to joy: "These things I have spoken to you, that My joy may be in you, and that your joy may be made full" (15:11). Even though the circumstances may be extremely adverse, the one who personally knows the God of joy and peace can have these qualities in his own life.

The Example of the Early Church

The believers in the early church had grasped this truth well. After the apostles had been flogged by the Sanhedrin for preaching the gospel, "they went on their way from the presence of the Council, rejoicing that they had been considered worthy to suffer shame for His name. And every day, in the temple and from house to house, they kept right on teaching and preaching Jesus as the Christ" (Acts 5:41,42).

When James wrote to the Jews scattered among the Gentiles, he said, "Consider it all joy, my brethren, when you encounter various trials, knowing that the testing of your faith produces endurance. And let endurance have its perfect result, that you may be perfect and complete, lacking in nothing" (James 1:2-4).

Peter, also writing primarily to Jewish believers, said, "Beloved, do not be surprised at the fiery ordeal among you, which comes upon you for your testing, as though some strange thing were happening to you; but to the degree that you share the sufferings of Christ, keep on rejoicing; so that also at the revelation of His glory, you may rejoice with exultation. If you are reviled for the name of Christ, you are blessed, because the Spirit of glory and of God rests upon you" (I Pet. 4:12-14).

Believers in the early church—and we today who know Jesus Christ personally—had an overwhelming reason to always rejoice. The reason is Christ's attitude toward the believer and the fact that nothing can separate him from Christ's love. This was expressed by Paul specifically in Romans 8:35-39: "Who shall separate us from the love of Christ? Shall tribulation, or distress, or persecution, or famine, or nakedness, or peril, or sword? Just as it is written, 'For Thy sake, we are being put to death all day long; we were considered as sheep to be slaughtered.' But in all these things we overwhelmingly conquer through Him who loved us. For I am convinced that neither death, nor life, nor angels, nor principalities, nor things present, nor things to come, nor powers, nor height, nor depth, nor any other created thing, shall be able to separate us from the love of God, which is in Christ Jesus our Lord."

How wonderful to know that Jesus Christ indwells every believer so we may rejoice under all circumstances because we are in Christ.

Chapter 2

Christ Our Life

In focusing attention on Philippians 1, it should be remembered that this chapter particularly emphasizes that Christ is everything to the believer. The phrase "for to me to live is Christ" (v. 21, KJV) sums up the attitude of Paul's heart as he wrote this significant letter to the believers in Philippi.

Right Relationship With Christ

Before treating the actual verses in the Book of Philippians, it is important to state what is meant by a right relationship with Christ not only concerning salvation but also concerning living a life of spiritual victory. That Christ is everything to the believer is also stated by Paul in Colossians 1:27: "Christ in you, the hope of glory." Salvation means that we have been united to Christ; that is, that we are one in Christ. Several verses of Scripture emphasize this truth. Ephesians 2:10 says, "For we are His workmanship, created in Christ Jesus for good works." The unity of believers with Christ is also seen in I Corinthians 12:13: "For by one Spirit we were all baptized into one body."

The Believer in Christ

What does it mean to be "in Christ"? This significant New Testament truth has two aspects: We are in Christ, and Christ is in us. These two aspects are seen in John 15:4: "Abide in Me, and I in you. As the branch cannot bear fruit of itself, unless it abides in the vine, so neither can you, unless you abide in Me."

That we are in Christ emphasizes that He is our entire life. Just as my arms are attached to my body so that the source of my life may flow to them, so also believers are in Christ so that His life may flow to them. God is the source of life, for the Bible says, "For just as the Father has life in Himself, even so He gave to the Son also to have life in Himself" (5:26).

We are told in I John 5:11,12 how to have eternal life: "And the witness is this, that God has given us eternal life, and this life is in His Son. He who has the Son has the life; he who does not have the Son of God does not have the life." That life is in Christ was one of the claims Jesus Himself made. He said, "I am the way, and the truth, and the life; no one comes to the Father, but through Me" (John 14:6).

Christ in the Believer

Not only is the believer in Christ, Christ is also in the believer and is the believer's source of activity, or daily service. This is especially emphasized in Colossians 1:27: "Christ in you, the hope of glory." Having stated that great truth, Paul went on to say, "And for this purpose also I labor, striving according to His power, which mightily works within me" (v. 29).

That Christ works mightily in the believer is especially seen in Philippians 2, in such verses as 5, 12 and 13. This will be especially emphasized when we study that portion of Philippians. Hebrews 13:21 refers to what God is personally doing: "Working in us that which is pleasing in His sight, through Jesus Christ." This is a sufficient number of verses to emphasize the teaching of the Scripture that the outworking of the indwelling Christ is our responsibility by the grace of God. This is what true spiritual life is all about—allowing the life of the indwelling Christ to be manifested through us in various ways. This will especially be seen in our study of Philippians 1.

The tremendous truth of Christ within us is taught in the Book of Romans, particularly in Chapter 8. The content of the Book of Philippians begins where Romans leaves off. Philippians assumes the proper doctrine and is concerned that the doctrine become a part of daily living. The truth of Christ within is the only place where the Christian experience can begin. The same truth is stated in different ways in the Bible.

Jesus told Nicodemus: "Unless one is born again, he cannot see the kingdom of God" (John 3:3). That Christ needs to be received as our life is seen in John 1:12,13: "But as many as received Him, to them He gave the right to become children of God, even to those who believe in His name, who were born not of blood, nor of the will of the flesh, nor of the will of man, but of God."

Concerning the way we become one with Christ, Titus 3:5 says, "He saved us, not on the basis of deeds which we have done in righteousness, but according to His mercy, by the washing of regeneration and renewing by the Holy Spirit."

Becoming united with Christ is spoken of in II Peter 1:4 as receiving His nature: "For by these He has granted to us His precious and magnificent promises, in order that by them you might become partakers of the divine nature, having escaped the corruption that is in the world by lust." The uniqueness of each person in Christ is emphasized in II Corinthians 5:17: "Therefore if any man is in Christ, he is a new creature; the old things passed away; behold, new things have come."

Faith Alone

All of this is experienced on the basis of faith and faith alone. No one can come into right relationship with Jesus Christ except by faith. The Bible clearly states: "For by grace you have been saved through faith; and that not of yourselves, it is the gift of God; not as a result of works, that no one should boast" (Eph. 2:8,9). Romans 4:5 says, "But to the one who does not work, but believes in Him who justifies the ungodly, his faith is reckoned as righteousness." Romans 5:1 further emphasizes the faith aspect: "Therefore having been justified by faith, we have peace with God through our Lord Jesus Christ."

A central passage of Scripture concerning how we become right with God is Romans 3:21-25: "But now apart from the Law the righteousness of God has been manifested, being witnessed by the Law and the Prophets; even the righteousness of God through faith in Jesus Christ for all those who believe; for there is no distinction; for all have sinned and fall short of the glory of God, being justified as a gift by His grace through the redemption which is in Christ Jesus; whom God displayed publicly as a propitiation in His blood through faith. This was to demonstrate His righteousness, because in the forbearance of God He passed over the sins previously committed."

So it is clear from the Scriptures that salvation is by faith in Christ alone. But some might be confused as to precisely what is meant by the word "faith." There seems to be two kinds of faith that are confused. The one kind I would simply call "historical faith." This kind of faith believes that Jesus Christ was a historical person; that is, that He lived on earth, died, rose again and ascended to heaven. But simply believing those facts does not change one's life any more than believing that Caesar lived years ago and accomplished many feats changes one's life. That is simply a historical faith.

The other kind of faith is what I call "saving faith." This is the faith by which a person realizes he is a sinner under condemnation and, realizing that Christ has paid the penalty for his sin, he places his trust in Christ as his personal Saviour. And by faith, that person can say, "Thank you, Lord, for coming into my life." As Christ becomes a part of the person's life, Christ's nature becomes his nature and Christ's life becomes his life. This is the beginning of the Christian experience and is what Philippians 1 talks about in detail and summarizes in verse 21: "For to me to live is Christ" (KJV).

In salvation, Christ imparts His life to us. Before that time, we were dead in trespasses and sins (see Eph. 2:1). But although we were dead in trespasses and sins, we now live by His life, having placed faith in Jesus Christ. He imparts Himself to us so He lives His life in us. Romans 5:10 emphasizes both Christ's death and life for us: "For if while we were enemies, we were reconciled to God through the death of His Son, much more, having been reconciled, we shall be saved by His life."

Christ's life in us is, for all practical purposes, the root of all of our living. This is what Paul expressed in Galatians 2:20: "I have been crucified with Christ; and it is no longer I who live, but Christ lives in me; and the life which I now live in the flesh I live by faith in the Son of God, who loved me, and delivered Himself up for me." This is why Paul also wrote: "As you therefore have received Christ Jesus the Lord, so walk in Him" (Col. 2:6).

From the moment of salvation forward, life takes on a new purpose and has a new focal point; believers are able to say with Paul, "For to me to live is Christ" (Phil. 1:21, KJV).

The Salutation

In the first verse of Paul's letter to the Philippians, he introduced himself and specifically mentioned to whom he was writing: "Paul and Timotheus, the servants of Jesus Christ, to all the saints in Christ Jesus which are at Philippi, with the bishops and deacons" (1:1, KJV).

From Paul and Timothy

In many of Paul's epistles he referred to himself as an apostle to show his authority for what he was writing. This was not necessary, however, as he wrote to the Philippians because Paul's authority was not in question. He did not have a criticism of them, so he did not have to exercise his authority. He put himself on an equal basis with those to whom he was writing and simply referred to himself and to Timothy as "servants of Jesus Christ."

The Greek word Paul used for "servants" was well known throughout the Roman Empire with its system of slavery. Paul's word was the plural form of the common word of that day that simply meant "slave." "Servant" is an acceptable translation if one realizes the strong meaning of the word.

Inasmuch as the believer is one who is bound to Christ willingly, this word is sometimes translated "bondslave" or "bondservant." That every believer belongs to Jesus Christ is clearly seen from I Corinthians 6:19,20: "Or do you not know that your body is a temple of the Holy Spirit who is in you, whom you have from God, and that you are not your own? For you have been bought with a price: therefore glorify God in your body."

When we believers take the attitude that we are bond-

slaves of the Lord Jesus Christ, this will influence our attitudes toward prayer, our relationship with others, our daily
lives and especially our relationship to Christ.

To the Saints at Philippi

Having said who the letter was from, Paul then said who
the letter was to: "To all the saints in Christ Jesus which are
at Philippi" (Phil. 1:1, KJV).

The Greek word Paul used for "saints" is related to other
such words as "holy" and "sanctified." The Greek words do
not refer to a state of sinless perfection but to a state of being
set apart to God. The one who trusts Jesus Christ as personal
Saviour is at that moment set apart to God.

Notice where Paul emphasized that these set apart ones
are—"in Christ Jesus." Here Paul was emphasizing the
union that each believer has with Jesus Christ. The words
"in Christ" or "in Christ Jesus" are distinctively characteristic of Church-Age believers. These terms are never used of
Old Testament believers or of believers after the Church
Age, such as during the Tribulation. That believers are in
Christ is indicated in I Corinthians 12:13: "For by one Spirit
we were all baptized into one body, whether Jews or Greeks,
whether slaves or free, and we were all made to drink of one
Spirit."

The Local Church and the Universal Church

But Paul was not writing to every person who was in
Christ Jesus; he was writing to those in Christ Jesus "which
are at Philippi" (Phil. 1:1, KJV). Believers all around the
world are part of the Body of Christ, or what is sometimes
known as the "universal Church." However, those believers
in a specific locality who are organized to minister to each
other are known as a "local church." The Bible is clear that
there is such an organization as a local church and that the
local church is the key means through which God wants to
work. But the local church should not be isolated and refuse
to recognize other believers in other local churches.

When the Church first began on the Day of Pentecost, the
Bible says, "So then, those who had received his word were

baptized; and there were added that day about three thousand souls" (Acts 2:41). These believers were not only united in Christ, but they were also part of the local church in Jerusalem. That this church was an evangelistic church is seen from verse 47: "The Lord was adding to their number day by day those who were being saved." Later, when Stephen was stoned to death in Jerusalem and Saul was in agreement with those who put him to death, the Bible says, "And on that day a great persecution arose against the church in Jerusalem; and they were all scattered throughout the regions of Judea and Samaria, except the apostles" (8:1). From this reference it is apparent there was a local church in Jerusalem because the believers there were referred to as "the church in Jerusalem."

I am committed to the importance of the local church and its ministry. My wife and I have always attended a local church and have taken an active part. In fact, in the local church where we attend, my wife has been teaching continuously for over 25 years. Our children grew up there, were baptized there and became members of that local church. From these things you can see that we strongly believe the local church is an exceedingly important means through which God works.

But our local church is not the only means; we have to recognize there are other local churches where there are born-again believers who are seriously involved in the study of the Word of God and are endeavoring to have an outreach in their community and to the world. Even in some local churches that are liberal in theology, we recognize there are some genuine believers who are doing what they can to honor the Lord. There are believers in local churches all over the world, and those who are involved in a particular local church need to recognize this fact and pray for them. However, I believe that each believer ought to be involved himself in a particular local church where he receives teaching from the Word of God and contributes to the spiritual lives of others and is involved in having an outreach to the community and to the world.

The local church is emphasized in such verses as I Timothy 3:15: "I write so that you may know how one ought to conduct himself in the household of God, which is the

church of the living God, the pillar and support of the truth."
All believers in the Body of Christ are emphasized in such
verses as I Corinthians 10:32: "Give no offense either to Jews
or to Greeks or to the church of God."

The universal Church, or the Church-at-large, is also
referred to in Hebrews 12:23: "To the general assembly and
church of the first-born who are enrolled in heaven." The
Church-at-large is that group which constitutes all believers
from the time of Pentecost until the return of the Lord Jesus
Christ, at which time believers will be raptured, or caught
up, to meet Him in the air.

The Church-at-large and those who comprise it are known
by various descriptions. Ephesians 2:15 refers to the Jews
and Gentiles and the Church-at-large as being "one new
man."

Ephesians 1:22,23 refers to the Church-at-large as the
Body of Christ: "And He put all things in subjection under
His feet, and gave Him as head over all things to the church,
which is His body, the fulness of Him who fills all in all." The
Church as Christ's Body is also referred to in Ephesians
5:30: "We are members of His body."

The Church-at-large is also known as the "Bride of Christ"
and as the "Lamb's wife." These expressions are derived
from Revelation 19:7 and 21:9: "Let us rejoice and be glad
and give the glory to Him, for the marriage of the Lamb has
come and His bride has made herself ready." "And one of the
seven angels who had the seven bowls full of the seven last
plagues, came and spoke with me, saying, 'Come here, I shall
show you the bride, the wife of the Lamb.' "

A distinction should also be kept in mind concerning the
Church-at-large and the local church. Only believers in
Jesus Christ are part of the Church-at-large, but in a local
church it is possible for unbelievers to attend and, regrettably, to sometimes even become members. But God recognizes
only those who are genuinely born again. As the Church Age
progresses, more and more unbelievers will take on the form
of godliness and attend local churches. This will produce an
apostate Christendom which will be judged during the Tribulation, according to Revelation 17 and 18.

In Paul's letter to the Philippians we see that the Philippian believers had a dual habitation. First, Paul said that the

believers were "in Christ Jesus," but he also spoke of them as being "at Philippi" (Phil. 1:1, KJV). Thus, we see that they were living in two places at the same time. Later in Paul's letter to the Philippians, he emphasized the same truth when he said, "For our citizenship is in heaven, from which also we eagerly wait for a Savior, the Lord Jesus Christ" (3:20). So although the believers to whom Paul was writing were living on earth in the city of Philippi, they were also citizens of heaven who were in Christ.

Grace and Peace

At the beginning of Paul's letter to the Philippians, he continued his salutation by saying, "Grace be unto you, and peace, from God our Father, and from the Lord Jesus Christ" (1:2, KJV).

Notice especially the words "grace" and "peace." The order in which these words occur is highly significant. It is never "peace and grace"; it is always "grace and peace." The difference is important because grace must come from God and be received before one can experience true peace. Until one becomes a child of God, it is impossible to talk of real peace. Isaiah 57:21 says, " 'There is no peace,' says my God, 'for the wicked.' "

Peace with God and the peace of God are possible only through salvation: "But now in Christ Jesus you who formerly were far off have been brought near by the blood of Christ. For He Himself is our peace, who made both groups into one, and broke down the barrier of the dividing wall" (Eph. 2:13,14). Notice especially the words "He Himself is our peace."

So God's order is first grace, then peace. It is as if God says to us, "You accept My grace, and I will give you My peace."

Paul's Concern Expressed

In verses 3-11 of Philippians 1, Paul told of his concern for his spiritual children. In a distinct sense, Paul was the founder of the local church in Philippi and was kind of a pastor-in-absence. No doubt they had a pastor, or pastors, but because of Paul's involvement in the beginning of the church there was a significant tie between Paul and the believers in Philippi.

Prayerful Remembrance With Joy

Paul told them, "I thank my God upon every remembrance of you" (Phil. 1:3, KJV). This is what might be called a "prayerful remembrance." Whenever the indwelling Christ reminded Paul of the believers in Philippi, he thanked God for them. Essentially, Paul was saying, "Whenever you come to my mind, I remember you with thanksgiving and prayer." Just as it was true in the case of the Apostle Paul, so it can be true today that the indwelling Christ reminds us of our prayer responsibility toward other members of the Body of Christ.

Paul continued: "Always in every prayer of mine for you all making request with joy" (v. 4, KJV). In other words, Paul was saying to the Philippians, "Whenever I pray for you, it is with joy."

Remember, Paul was writing from a Roman imprisonment, and the church to which he was writing, in a sense, had its birth in prison. But Paul was full of joy whenever he thought about, and prayed for, the Philippian believers.

The Christian's life is a life that is in Christ, and it is always characterized by joy when Christ is in control. Although happiness depends on what happens, a Christian can always have joy because of his relationship to Jesus Christ. As we will see later from Philippians, Paul's attitude was one of forgetting past circumstances and looking ahead to all that Jesus Christ had in store for him (see 3:13).

In this regard, there is no reason for the believer to be gloomy. He needs to realize that he is united with the Lord Jesus Christ, who gives His peace to all who believe in Him. As Jesus told His disciples, "These things I have spoken to you, that in Me you may have peace. In the world you have tribulation, but take courage; I have overcome the world" (John 16:33).

Paul indicated he had made requests for the Philippians with joy (v. 4), but what was the reason for his joy? The answer is in the following verse: "For your fellowship in the gospel from the first day until now" (v. 5, KJV). From the very first day the Philippians had heard the good news of the gospel, they had been cooperating with Paul in spreading this good news.

When a person becomes a Christian and is united in heart and life with Jesus Christ, he also becomes united with others who are furthering the work of Christ in proclaiming the good news. Believers are to work together as a single unit—as one living body. We are not only to be working with each other; we are also to be working with God. Paul told the Corinthians: "For we are God's fellow-workers" (I Cor. 3:9).

That we are to perform together as one body is evident from I Corinthians 12:12: "For even as the body is one and yet has many members, and all the members of the body, though they are many, are one body, so also is Christ." So believers are to function together as a single unit as the Body of Christ, with Christ Himself superintending the activity of the various members.

God's Good Work

Having referred to the reason for his joy as he remembered the Philippians, Paul said, "Being confident of this very thing, that he which hath begun a good work in you will perform it until the day of Jesus Christ" (Phil. 1:6, KJV). Notice particularly that the work of God is begun "in" a person. Many people think of the work of God that is done through them, but God cannot work *through* us until He has worked *in* us. Because God had done such a tremendous work in Paul, he was able to say, "For to me to live is Christ" (v. 21, KJV). It is also the believer's responsibility to work out of his life what God has worked into his life (see 2:12,13).

From all of this we see that the spiritual life is God's undertaking. Once we know Jesus Christ as our life and recognize that all of life is to be lived by and for Him, then it becomes His undertaking to see us through. And what He has begun in us, He will finish.

This is the same truth emphasized in Romans 8:28,29: "And we know that God causes all things to work together for good to those who love God, to those who are called according to His purpose. For whom He foreknew, He also predestined to become conformed to the image of His Son,

that He might be the first-born among many brethren."
What God begins, He completes.

This does not mean that we are to take a passive attitude,
as if to say, "Well, if He's going to do it, I don't have to do
anything." This is missing the point the Scripture makes.
We are to cooperate with Jesus Christ. He is working in us to
accomplish a specific work so we can then work it out
through our lives. This is why He allows certain things to
come into our lives in order to accomplish His work in us, so
we have something to work out in our lives that will be of
benefit to others.

Sometimes we become discouraged and disgruntled and
even have a bad attitude toward the Lord Himself. It is
characteristic of the Lord at times like these to do something
so wonderful for us that He breaks our hearts with His
kindness. I used to work with a person who became upset
easily and who would get very aggravated at someone. Then
I would see him weep after such an experience as he was
made to realize the goodness of the Lord. He would say, "You
know, the Lord always meets me with such wonderful love
and compassion, it breaks my heart because of the way I
treat Him." Truly, God is working all things together for our
good and His glory, and what He begins in us He is going to
complete.

Interrelationships

Verses 7 and 8 of Philippians 1 tell of the interrelationships Paul and the Philippians had because they possessed
the same spiritual life. Paul wrote: "Even as it is meet for me
to think this of you all, because I have you in my heart;
inasmuch as both in my bonds, and in the defence and
confirmation of the gospel, ye all are partakers of my grace.
For God is my record, how greatly I long after you all in the
bowels of Jesus Christ" (1:7,8, KJV).

The Philippians stood by Paul whether he was out preaching the gospel or confined in prison. They were "partakers"
of his grace (v. 7); that is, they had shared together in the
grace Paul had experienced.

In the human sense, it took a lot of grace on Paul's part to
live under the kind of circumstances he did and still be able

to live victoriously. Let us never forget, however, that the entire Christian life is lived by God's grace. And we have received all the grace we need to live victoriously. John 1:16 says, "For of His fulness we have all received, and grace upon grace." Ephesians 4:7 says, "But to each one of us grace was given according to the measure of Christ's gift." Because of the grace we have received, grace is available in every trial and need. "God is able to make all grace abound to you, that always having all sufficiency in everything, you may have an abundance for every good deed" (II Cor. 9:8).

The Christ-filled believer has the inner feeling of compassion for those of like faith. It is kind of an inner homesickness—a spiritual longing for other members of the Body. In this regard I often think of missionaries who labor in new fields of ministry where there are no Christians. How lonely they get because there are no believers with whom they can share their burdens.

On the other hand, many in North America claim to be believers and yet do not go to church. They say, "One does not need to go to church to be a Christian." Technically that is true, but one indication that a person is a Christian is that he wants to be with others who are related to Christ. The Bible says, "Not forsaking our own assembling together, as is the habit of some, but encouraging one another; and all the more, as you see the day drawing near" (Heb. 10:25). Colossians 3:16 says, "Let the word of Christ richly dwell within you, with all wisdom teaching and admonishing one another with psalms and hymns and spiritual songs, singing with thankfulness in your hearts to God." So we need fellowship with others who know Christ in order that we might build each other up in the faith and go back out to meet the world and to proclaim the gospel.

Prayer for Spiritual Growth

In verses 9-11 of Philippians 1, Paul prayed for the spiritual growth of the Philippian believers. "And this I pray, that your love may abound yet more and more in knowledge and in all judgment; that ye may approve things that are excellent; that ye may be sincere and without offence till the day of Christ; being filled with the fruits of righteousness,

which are by Jesus Christ, unto the glory and praise of God"
(KJV).

This prayer is in sharp contrast with what Paul said to the
Corinthians: "And I, brethren, could not speak to you as to
spiritual men, but as to men of flesh, as to babes in Christ. I
gave you milk to drink, not solid food; for you were not yet
able to receive it. Indeed, even now you are not yet able, for
you are still fleshly. For since there is jealousy and strife
among you, are you not fleshly, and are you not walking like
mere men?" (I Cor. 3:1-3).

Also, the writer to the Hebrews (quite possibly Paul) had to
tell his readers: "For though by this time you ought to be
teachers, you have need again for some one to teach you the
elementary principles of the oracles of God, and you have
come to need milk and not solid food. For every one who
partakes only of milk is not accustomed to the word of righteousness, for he is a babe. But solid food is for the mature,
who because of practice have their senses trained to discern
good and evil" (Heb. 5:12-14).

Abounding Love

Paul wanted the love of the Philippians to abound in
"knowledge and in all judgment" (Phil. 1:9, KJV). The Greek
word Paul used for "knowledge" was an intensive form of
the common word for knowledge. This intensive form referred
to an advanced knowledge. Paul did not want the Philippians
to remain at their present level of knowledge of the Lord, as
good as that level might have been for them at that time. He
wanted them to advance in their knowledge of Jesus Christ,
and he wanted their love to be expressed in accordance with
this knowledge.

Paul was also concerned that the love of the Philippians
might abound "in all judgment." The Greek word translated
"judgment" means "insight." It has to do with the application of knowledge, which results in discernment. Christians
who are unable to discern are not mature and thus are not
able to handle the solid food of the Word.

Paul wanted the Philippians to have depth of insight and
more comprehensive discernment. So we see from Philippians 1:9 that it is not enough to know factual information

from the Bible; one must apply this information to himself
and to the situations in which he finds himself.

Paul was particularly concerned that the Philippians
approve that which was of real value. Each believer needs to
ask himself, "What are my values?" We are living in a time
of strong materialistic attitudes, and Christians can be
easily affected by them. It is important that believers put
first things first and not be affected by the things of this
world rather than having their eyes on eternal values. Of
course, the first thing in our lives should be Jesus Christ
Himself. This was the case with the Apostle Paul, and that's
why he was able to say, "For to me to live is Christ" (1:21,
KJV).

Fruit of Righteousness

Paul's desire for the Philippians is revealed in Philippians
1:11: "Being filled with the fruits of righteousness, which are
by Jesus Christ, unto the glory and praise of God." Notice the
expression "fruits [literally, fruit] of righteousness." This
refers to the results of righteousness which Paul was concerned would be manifested in the lives of the Philippians.

It is important to distinguish between righteousness and
the fruit of righteousness. We do not produce righteousness
in order to receive salvation. Righteousness for salvation
comes by faith, as stated in Romans 3:21,22: "But now apart
from the Law the righteousness of God has been manifested,
being witnessed by the Law and the Prophets, even the
righteousness of God through faith in Jesus Christ for all
those who believe; for there is no distinction." Also, Romans
10:4 states, "For Christ is the end of the law for righteousness to everyone who believes." So righteousness for salvation is found only in Christ and is available only by grace
through faith.

However, the *fruit* of righteousness is our labor in Him;
that is, our activities that glorify Him. God works in us to
cause us to be willing to do His good pleasure (Phil. 2:12,13),
and as we manifest good works that glorify Him, we produce
the fruit of righteousness.

Concerning expressing righteousness, the Apostle John
said, "Little children, let no one deceive you; the one who

practices righteousness is righteous, just as He is righteous" (I John 3:7). So the indication, or proof, that a person is righteous is that he does those things which are characteristic of righteousness. Verse 10 states the same truth negatively: "By this the children of God and the children of the devil are obvious: any one who does not practice righteousness is not of God, nor the one who does not love his brother." So the person who is righteous because he has trusted Jesus Christ as Saviour will do righteous acts; he will produce the fruit of righteousness.

We are reminded from I John 5:1,4 that the doing comes from the being: "Whoever believes that Jesus is the Christ is born of God; and whoever loves the Father loves the child born of Him. . . . For whatever is born of God overcomes the world; and this is the victory that has overcome the world—our faith." So the one who is born again will love others who are born again. When we are righteous, we will evidence the characteristics of righteousness.

Notice the source of the fruit of righteousness in Philippians 1:11: "Which are by Jesus Christ" (KJV). The fruit of righteousness originates with Christ, not in the believer's self-efforts. This is why Paul said, "For to me to live is Christ" (v. 21, KJV).

That Christ works in the believer to accomplish a significant work is seen also from Colossians 1:29: "And for this purpose also I labor, striving according to His power, which mightily works within me." Hebrews 13:20,21 also reveals the work of God in a believer: "Now the God of peace, who brought up from the dead the great Shepherd of the sheep through the blood of the eternal covenant, even Jesus our Lord, equip you in every good thing to do His will, working in us that which is pleasing in His sight, through Jesus Christ, to whom be the glory forever and ever. Amen."

When we are righteous, we will produce the fruit of righteousness.

Paul the Prisoner

Verses 12-30 of Philippians 1 especially set forth Paul's situation as a prisoner—the things that happened to him in this state and the confidence he had for the future. Although

Paul was a prisoner of Rome, his own attitude was that of a free man because he considered himself in reality to be a bondslave of Jesus Christ. Paul realized that the Word of God could not be bound, so he did not consider himself to be bound. The only person to whom Paul was bound was Jesus Christ; therefore, Paul's supreme concern for the gospel outweighed all other considerations. As a result, Paul experienced victory instead of gloom. This can be true of every Christian whose life is taken up with Jesus Christ because such a believer can triumph, by faith, over all circumstances. There is no suggestion in Philippians of defeat in Paul's life, and there need not be in your life or mine.

Paul's all-consuming passion for Jesus Christ is a reminder of what he said in Galatians 2:20: "I have been crucified with Christ; and it is no longer I who live, but Christ lives in me; and the life which I now live in the flesh I live by faith in the Son of God, who loved me, and delivered Himself up for me."

Paul's victorious attitude can be ours because the same Christ indwells us. Hebrews 13:8 reminds us: "Jesus Christ is the same yesterday and today, yes and forever."

Advancing the Gospel

Paul told the Philippians, "But I would ye should understand, brethren, that the things which happened unto me have fallen out rather unto the furtherance of the gospel" (Phil. 1:12, KJV).

The gospel had been advanced. Progress had been made on every side, even though Paul was bound physically. A study of Paul's imprisonment indicates that the time he was writing to the Philippians coincides with his imprisonment recorded in Acts 28. Verses 30 and 31 state, "And he stayed two full years in his own rented quarters, and was welcoming all who came to him, preaching the kingdom of God, and teaching concerning the Lord Jesus Christ with all openness, unhindered." Even though Paul was probably bound to a Roman soldier wherever he went, he at least had freedom to move about and had boldness in Christ to preach the gospel wherever he went. Apparently there were several conversions right within Caesar's household because in concluding his letter to the Philippians, Paul said, "All the saints greet you, especially those of Caesar's household" (4:22).

Reference to Caesar's household is also made in Philippians 1:13: "So that my bonds in Christ are manifest in all the palace, and in all other places" (KJV). In this verse, Paul seemed to glory in his bonds. He realized that this had brought an advance to the gospel which might not otherwise have been possible. Had it not been for his imprisonment, it is extremely unlikely that Caesar's palace guards would have heard the good news of salvation. No wonder Paul was able to say, "We know that God causes all things to work together for good to those who love God, to those who are called according to His purpose" (Rom. 8:28).

Paul's imprisonment also had an effect on other believers. Paul said, "And many of the brethren in the Lord, waxing confident by my bonds, are much more bold to speak the word without fear" (Phil. 1:14, KJV).

It was apparently dangerous to preach the gospel in Rome because the authorities were always checking on those who might be doing so. But instead of Paul's imprisonment causing the other believers to be more afraid of preaching the gospel, they were greatly encouraged and spoke out even more boldly for the Lord. They were acting with more freedom and were more indifferent to the consequences that might come to them.

Paul's fearlessness even in bonds and his triumph in spite of imprisonment caused fellow believers to see Christ's power in him and to realize that the same power was available to them because the same Christ indwelt them.

Paul went on to say, "Some indeed preach Christ even of envy and strife; and some also of good will: the one preach Christ of contention, not sincerely, supposing to add affliction to my bonds: but the other of love, knowing that I am set for the defence of the gospel" (vv. 15-17, KJV).

Even though some were preaching the gospel out of a party spirit instead of from pure motives, Paul rejoiced that the gospel was being preached. His response to all of this was: "What then? Notwithstanding, every way, whether in pretence, or in truth, Christ is preached; and I therein do rejoice, yea, and will rejoice" (v. 18, KJV).

Only a person who has clearly grasped the truth of "Christ

in you, the hope of glory" (Col. 1:27) can have the kind of peace that Paul had even in confinement. Such peace is referred to even in the Old Testament. Psalm 119:165 says, "Those who love Thy law have great peace, and nothing causes them to stumble."

Magnifying Christ

Having told the Philippians that he rejoiced that Christ was preached, regardless of the motives of the preachers, Paul said, "For I know that this shall turn to my salvation through your prayer, and the supply of the Spirit of Jesus Christ, according to my earnest expectation and my hope, that in nothing I shall be ashamed, but that with all boldness, as always, so now also Christ shall be magnified in my body, whether it be by life, or by death" (Phil. 1:19,20, KJV).

The life of the indwelling Christ enabled Paul to be free from worry and self-care during his imprisonment, which could have led to death. Paul was bold and unashamed and was concerned only that Christ would be magnified in his body regardless of what awaited him—life or death. There was no wavering on his part.

We tend to think that these tremendous qualities were true only of the great men of God, like the Apostle Paul, but that it is impossible for us to attain them. Somehow Satan blinds our eyes to the fact that we can have the same determination to glorify Christ in our lives that Paul had in his. The same Christ indwells us not only to give us the desire to glorify Him but also to enable us to have the boldness to carry out that desire.

Having told of his desire to please Christ in everything, whether through life or through death, Paul said, "For to me to live is Christ, and to die is gain" (v. 21, KJV). This was the basis for Paul's being able to live victoriously in Christ. He was not concerned about drawing attention to himself; rather, he wanted to glorify Jesus Christ in everything. All of Paul's life was focused on Jesus Christ.

It is good for each of us to weigh his or her activities and ask, "Are the things I am doing all done to further my own interests, or are they really glorifying Christ?" It is also good for us to ask, "Can I really say with Paul, 'For to me, to live is Christ, and to die is gain'?" (v. 21).

Notice that two specific aspects are mentioned in verse 21—life and death. Whatever Paul did in this life, he wanted to count for Jesus Christ and not just to live for selfish interests. He expressed the same thought in different words in Galatians 2:20: "It is no longer I who live, but Christ lives in me; and the life which I now live in the flesh I live by faith in the Son of God, who loved me, and delivered Himself up for me."

Consider the death aspect of Paul's statement in Philippians 1:21. Think of what it would be like to be able to say, "To die is gain." Paul had such a close relationship with Jesus Christ that he felt it would be a personal advantage to pass from this life and to be in the presence of Jesus Christ. Paul realized at this time, however, that God had other plans for him.

Paul told the Philippians, "But if I live in the flesh, this is the fruit of my labour: yet what I shall choose I wot not. For I am in a strait betwixt two, having a desire to depart, and to be with Christ; which is far better: nevertheless to abide in the flesh is more needful for you" (vv. 22-24, KJV).

After analyzing his situation, Paul realized that even though it would be a personal advantage to be in the presence of Christ, he still had a purpose for serving the Lord here on earth. At the time he was writing these words he was in confinement with the possibility of a cruel death awaiting him at the hands of the Roman government. Yet he could say it was better for him to remain on earth instead of going to be with the Lord because of what it meant to the believers in Philippi.

Paul had endured many severe experiences in the intervening ten years since he had founded the church in Philippi. An enumeration of many of them is given in II Corinthians 11:24-28. Read that passage of Scripture and let the details sink deeply into your mind. Paul had undergone so much already, and yet he was convinced that the believers in Philippi needed him so much that it would be better for him to be on earth than to be in the presence of Jesus Christ. He realized this in spite of the fact that he well knew that he would experience more suffering and probably even death at the hands of his persecutors. What a tremendous man he was; no, rather, what a tremendous God he had—and we have the same God!

Example of Jonah

In the light of Paul's determination to please God in everything, whether by life or by death, it is especially interesting to note two examples of Old Testament prophets who serve as contrasts to Paul's attitude.

One such prophet was Jonah. God commanded him to go to Nineveh, the capital of the Assyrian Empire, to proclaim a message of repentance (see Jon. 1). However, Jonah realized that if the Assyrians were spared, they would most likely come against Israel and take it captive. So Jonah did not want Nineveh spared, he wanted it judged. He tried to escape his obligation, and the short Book of Jonah tells the vivid story. Finally, because there was no other alternative, Jonah did preach the message of repentance to the people of Nineveh, and the city did turn to God and was spared (see ch. 3). Jonah was greatly disappointed that God spared the capital of the Assyrian Empire, and the end of the Book of Jonah tells us how he went out of the city, made a shelter for himself and sat under it in self-pity (see ch. 4). God caused a plant to grow up over Jonah to shade him, and Jonah was extremely happy about the comfort he had from the burning, midday sun.

Notice, however, how the Book of Jonah concludes: "But God appointed a worm when dawn came the next day, and it attacked the plant and it withered. And it came about when the sun came up that God appointed a scorching east wind, and the sun beat down on Jonah's head so that he became faint and begged with all his soul to die, saying, 'Death is better to me than life.' Then God said to Jonah, 'Do you have good reason to be angry about the plant?' And he said, 'I have good reason to be angry, even to death.' Then the Lord said, 'You had compassion on the plant for which you did not work, and which you did not cause to grow, which came up overnight and perished overnight. And should I not have compassion on Nineveh, the great city in which there are more than 120,000 persons who do not know the difference

between their right and left hand, as well as many animals?' "
(vv. 7-11).

In contrast to the Apostle Paul, Jonah was without compassion for those who so desperately needed his message.
Jonah was compassionate for his own people, the Israelites,
but he had no compassion for the enemies of Israel and did
not even want to see them come to the Lord and be spared
judgment. In spite of Jonah's indifference, God brought a
revival to Nineveh, and the city was spared.

Each of us who knows Christ as Saviour needs to ask
himself, "Do I really want to see terrible sinners turned to
Christ and be spared judgment, or would I rather have them
remain in their unsaved state so they will experience the
judgment of God?" Each of us needs to check his own heart
in this regard.

Example of Elijah

Another Old Testament prophet who serves as a contrast
to the Apostle Paul is Elijah. Elijah was a wonderful man of
God and had a significant victory over the prophets of Baal
on Mount Carmel (I Kings 18:20-40). When Jezebel heard
that Elijah had killed the prophets of Baal, she sent a
message to Elijah: "So may the gods do to me and even more,
if I do not make your life as the life of one of them by
tomorrow about this time" (19:2).

Notice the response of this man of God, who had experienced such a tremendous victory: "He was afraid and arose
and ran for his life and came to Beersheba, which belongs to
Judah, and left his servant there. But he himself went a
day's journey into the wilderness, and came and sat down
under a juniper tree; and he requested for himself that he
might die, and said, 'It is enough; now, O Lord, take my life,
for I am not better than my fathers' " (vv. 3,4).

Elijah was sustained by the Lord at this time, and then he
went on to Horeb. When the Lord asked him what he was
doing there, Elijah answered, "I have been very zealous for
the Lord, the God of hosts; for the sons of Israel have for-
saken Thy covenant, torn down Thine alters and killed Thy
prophets with the sword. And I alone am left; and they seek
my life, to take it away" (v. 10).

Elijah was not the only one left, but I focus attention on his time of despair to show what a contrast he was to the Apostle Paul. Both Jonah and Elijah wanted to die, but although Paul knew it would be better to be in the presence of Christ, he realized God still had things for him to accomplish in this life. And if we allow Christ to have control of us as He did of the Apostle Paul, we will be more positive and triumphant, even in times of extremely troubling circumstances.

Submitting to God's Will

Having told the Philippians, "Nevertheless to abide in the flesh is more needful for you" (Phil. 1:24, KJV), Paul said, "And having this confidence, I know that I shall abide and continue with you all for your furtherance and joy of faith; that your rejoicing may be more abundant in Jesus Christ for me by my coming to you again" (vv. 25,26, KJV). Paul put aside any selfish interest and considered God's future for him to be his will also and rejoiced in it all.

This is a reminder of what Paul had said earlier, as recorded in Acts 20. At this time he was planning to go to Jerusalem, where possible imprisonment and perhaps even death awaited him. But in face of all of this, Paul made this triumphant statement: "But I do not consider my life of any account as dear to myself, in order that I may finish my course, and the ministry which I received from the Lord Jesus, to testify solemnly of the gospel of the grace of God" (v. 24).

Many of us ought to be ashamed of ourselves because of the grumbling we do over minor difficulties. Those observing us might wonder what we are living for. Are we really living for Christ and Him alone?

Suffering for Christ

Having assured the Philippians of his confidence that he would remain to be of help to them, Paul said, "Only let your conversation [conduct] be as it becometh the gospel of Christ: that whether I come and see you, or else be absent, I may hear of your affairs, that ye stand fast in one spirit, with one mind striving together for the faith of the gospel" (Phil. 1:27, KJV).

If Christ is our life, it will be reflected in our conduct. Paul was concerned that the Philippians' manner of life would be that which would honor Jesus Christ. He wanted their lives to measure up to the gospel of Christ. This was possible for the Philippians because the same Christ who lived on earth lived in them—and He also lives in us who have trusted Him as Saviour.

Paul was especially concerned that the Philippian believers "stand fast in one spirit, with one mind striving together for the faith of the gospel" (v. 27, KJV). All of us who are in Jesus Christ need to have our minds set on the same goal—to honor Jesus Christ in everything. As we work together, we should be like a team of athletes which functions as a single individual to accomplish the victory.

Paul added: "And in nothing terrified by your adversaries: which is to them an evident token of perdition, but to you of salvation, and that of God" (v. 28, KJV).

Paul was concerned that the believers in Philippi not be intimidated by their antagonists. Another translation renders the verse this way: "And do not [for a moment] be frightened or intimidated in anything by your opponents and adversaries, for such [constancy and fearlessness] will be a clear sign (proof and seal) to them of [their impending] destruction; but [a sure token and evidence] of your deliverance and salvation, and that from God" (Amplified).

Paul reminded the Philippian believers, "For unto you it is given in the behalf of Christ, not only to believe on him, but also to suffer for his sake" (v. 29, KJV).

Suffering for Christ is a part of the Christian's life; this is something that should never be forgotten. But it should also be remembered that a double honor is extended to those who suffer. To believe means life; to suffer means reward. When the apostles had been beaten for preaching the gospel and then released, "they went on their way from the presence of the Council, rejoicing that they had been considered worthy to suffer shame for His name" (Acts 5:41).

When Paul wrote to Timothy, he reminded him—and all believers—that "all who desire to live godly in Christ Jesus will be persecuted" (II Tim. 3:12). But do not forget Paul's statement made previously in the same letter: "If we endure, we shall also reign with Him" (2:12).

James wrote: "Blessed is a man who perseveres under trial; for once he has been approved, he will receive the crown of life, which the Lord has promised to those who love Him" (James 1:12).

On the subject of suffering, Peter said, "For this finds favor, if for the sake of conscience toward God a man bears up under sorrows when suffering unjustly. For what credit is there if, when you sin and are harshly treated, you endure it with patience? But if when you do what is right and suffer for it you patiently endure it, this finds favor with God. For you have been called for this purpose, since Christ also suffered for you, leaving you an example for you to follow in His steps, who committed no sin, nor was any deceit found in His mouth; and while being reviled, He did not revile in return; while suffering, He uttered no threats, but kept entrusting Himself to Him who judges righteously" (I Pet. 2:19-23).

In the same epistle, Peter said, "Beloved, do not be surprised at the fiery ordeal among you, which comes upon you for your testing, as though some strange thing were happening to you; but to the degree that you share the sufferings of Christ, keep on rejoicing; so that also at the revelation of His glory, you may rejoice with exaltation" (4:12,13).

Peter told all believers: "If anyone suffers as a Christian, let him not feel ashamed, but in that name let him glorify God. . . . Therefore, let those also who suffer according to the will of God entrust their souls to a faithful Creator in doing what is right" (vv. 16,19).

Having told the Philippian believers that they were destined to suffer for the sake of Christ, Paul told them: "Having the same conflict which ye saw in me, and now hear to be in me" (Phil. 1:30, KJV).

Paul had set an example for the Philippians in suffering. The first time they met him, it was in the context of a prison experience in Philippi (Acts 16). Ten years later he wrote as a prisoner of Rome, and during those intervening ten years he had suffered many things. So as the Philippians suffered, they would be well aware of the fact that they were not the only ones experiencing suffering for the cause of Jesus Christ.

Chapter 3

Christ Our Mind

Having seen that Christ is our life, as presented in Philippians 1, we now turn our attention to Philippians 2, where we discover that Christ is also to be our mind. Once we realize that "to me to live is Christ" (1:21, KJV), we need to heed the injunction: "Let this mind be in you, which was also in Christ Jesus" (2:5, KJV).

The Mind of Christ

The mind has to do with the mental attitude of the believer, which is to reflect his position in Christ. We are to keep on fostering the same disposition that Jesus Christ had.

Although Jesus Christ is our example in this regard, it is important to realize that He is much more than our example. There is a sense in which it is impossible to imitate Him. In order for His mind to be in us, it is necessary that He actually become our life, not just that we pattern our lives after Him. This is what Paul had in mind when he said, "For to me to live is Christ" (Phil. 1:21, KJV). Paul was not simply living the way he thought Christ might have lived; he was allowing Christ to live His life through him.

Paul told believers: "Work out your own salvation" (2:12, KJV). However, the clue to what Paul meant is in verse 13: "For it is God which worketh in you" (KJV). When the indwelling Christ performs His work in our lives, it is then our responsibility to work this out through our lives. We are to open the doors of our lives and let out what Christ has accomplished within us.

The roots of the Christian life are centered in Jesus Christ.

46

He came to earth, lived among men, died a man's death, was
raised to become our life, now lives in heaven to sustain our
life and is coming again to receive us out of this world. He is
the foundation upon which all else is based. Paul said, "For
no man can lay a foundation other than the one which is
laid, which is Jesus Christ" (I Cor. 3:11). Colossians 2:7
conveys the same idea: "Having been firmly rooted and now
being built up in Him and established in your faith."

But what determined the direction of Christ's life? Although different aspects might be mentioned, the key element was His mind. If he had not been humble in mind, He
would never have been humble in life. It was His manner of
thinking, therefore, that was so tremendously important as
He came to earth to live among men and to give His life on
the cross for the sin of the world. Our need is to think like
Christ thought, and we are helped in this because He
indwells us to think His thoughts through us.

Before the foundation of the world the Heavenly Father
planned all of this, and the Son set His mind to accomplish
all of it for us. In a sense, the mind of Christ was the starting
point from which all of His activities flowed.

Because the mind is so important Paul emphasized it in
his letter to the Philippians. The mind is referred to in different ways 12 times in the four chapters of Philippians. In
Chapter 1 is a reference to "one mind" (v. 27, KJV). In
Chapter 2 are expressions such as "like-minded" and "one
mind" (v. 2, KJV), "lowliness of mind" (v. 3, KJV) and "let
this mind be in you, which was also in Christ Jesus" (v. 5,
KJV). We will observe other expressions concerning the
mind throughout our study.

It is important to be aware that the mind can be either
fleshly or spiritual, according to the attitude that is dominant in our lives. Each believer should ask himself, Am I
filling my mind with things that are fleshly, even sensual?
Or am I letting the truths of the Word of God and Christ
Himself control my mind?

The Gospel accounts tell of the words and works of Jesus,
which reveal His character. However, in the Book of Philippians we read about the mind of Christ, which determined
His words and His works. Inasmuch as the way He thought
prompted what He said and did, it is important that we learn

how He thought so that we might think in the same way. "Let this mind be in you" (v. 5, KJV).

Since Philippians 2 especially emphasizes the mind of Christ, three aspects about Christ should be observed. First, note His mental attitude: "Who, being in the form of God, thought it not robbery to be equal with God" (v. 6, KJV). Second, note the activity springing out of that attitude: "But made himself of no reputation, and took upon him the form of a servant, and was made in the likeness of men: and being found in fashion as a man, he humbled himself, and became obedient unto death, even the death of the cross" (vv. 7,8, KJV). Third, note the victory and crowning of Jesus that resulted from His activity: "Wherefore God also hath highly exalted him, and given him a name which is above every name: that at the name of Jesus every knee should bow, of things in heaven, and things in earth, and things under the earth; and that every tongue should confess that Jesus Christ is Lord, to the glory of God the Father" (vv. 9-11, KJV).

So the crowning of Christ resulted from the activities of Christ which resulted from the mind of Christ. In order for us to know the mind of Christ, we must observe the activities of Christ because they reveal His manner of thinking. Although we cannot look into His mind, we can observe His activities, and in this way we can determine how He thought.

In Christ there was a proper order of all things, and we can experience the same only as we first acknowledge His indwelling and then His living out His life in us. As we allow Him to live out His life through us, we will do those things that honor Him because they will result from thinking which honors Him.

Identification With Christ

Consider the resources of the believer in all of this. Christ is his life, as seen from Paul's expression: "For to me to live is Christ" (Phil. 1:21, KJV). And Christ is the believer's mind: "Let this mind be in you, which was also in Christ Jesus" (2:5, KJV).

How can we appropriate all of this for ourselves? Is it by imitating Christ? No, that in itself will not do it. Is it by cultivating a better life, determining to do the best we can? No, that's not the answer either. How then can we appropriate the resources we have in Christ? By simply entering into the meaning that "to me to live is Christ" (1:21, KJV).

We must come to the place that Paul did so we can say, "I only have one life, and that is Christ." This is what led Paul to say, "I have been crucified with Christ; and it is no longer I who live, but Christ lives in me" (Gal. 2:20). Because Paul was so consumed with Christ he said, "I do not consider my life of any account as dear to myself, in order that I may finish my course, and the ministry which I received from the Lord Jesus" (Acts 20:24).

If we would have the mind of Christ, we must have the life of Christ, which is obtained not by imitation but by identification. That is what being born again means. Having trusted Him as our Saviour, we become identified with Him and He with us.

As we consider what all is involved in the mind of Christ, let us reflect a little on the Christ of history. Jesus Christ is the most outstanding figure of all time, so the question each person must answer is, What do I think about Jesus Christ?

As to His origin, Isaiah prophesied that He is "like a root out of parched ground" (Isa. 53:2). His life is unexplainable in the natural realm. History could not produce such a person. He came from outside of history during one of the world's darkest moments, and He will come again at another of the world's darkest moments.

During His life, Jesus spoke as no one ever had. He set forth a standard of life unknown to the finest minds of any age. His teachings are still the standard of the major philosophies of our day. No philosophy of our day has anything greater to present than the teachings of Jesus, but when Jesus Christ was here, He lived by them. Most people of the present age do not. He alone lived up to the perfect standard. After nearly 2000 years, not a single person has arisen to measure up to the standards of Jesus Christ.

He was not a mere man; He was the Saviour of mankind. But each person needs to personally receive Jesus Christ in order for the salvation He accomplished to be applied to that person's account. John 1:12 says, "As many as received Him, to them He gave the right to become children of God, even to those who believe in His name." John 5:24 says, "He who hears My word, and believes Him who sent Me, has eternal life, and does not come into judgment, but has passed out of death into life."

When we receive Jesus Christ as personal Saviour, He becomes our example, but He is much more than that—He is our life.

Someone might wonder, How was it possible for Christ to be all that He was? Of course, He was God Himself, but He did what He did as a result of His manner of thinking. He had a humble mind, He put others before Himself, and He planned our redemption even before we were created. If He had not been humble in His thinking, He never would have been humble in His living.

In a sense, we cannot imitate Him, we can only acquire Him by trusting Him as our Lord and Saviour and letting Him into our lives to take control of us and to live His life out through ours. This is why Paul said, "Let this mind be in you, which was also in Christ Jesus" (Phil. 2:5, KJV). All of Philippians 2 revolves around this verse as Paul emphasized to the Philippians the importance of having the mind of Christ. We are to let, or allow, Christ to control our minds because this is the basis of a productive, fruit-bearing Christian life.

Exhortation to One-Mindedness

Philippians 2 begins with Paul's words: "If there be therefore any consolation in Christ, if any comfort of love, if any fellowship of the Spirit, if any bowels and mercies" (v. 1, KJV).

This one verse contains four "if" clauses, and it is important to understand the significance of these clauses in the Greek language in which Paul was writing to the Philippians. In English, "if" presents a condition that may or may not be true. In the original language of this verse, however, the way the "if" clauses are used assumes the condition to be true. So one could read this verse, "If there be therefore any consolation in Christ, and there is," or "Because there is consolation in Christ."

Notice also in verse 1 the word "therefore," which refers to something previously said. In this case, it refers to what had been said in Chapter 1, particularly to Paul's statement in verse 21: "For to me to live is Christ" (KJV). And since Christ indwells every believer, this is the rich spiritual resource from which flows Christian experience and fellowship.

Consider further the four "ifs" in verse 1. Remember, because of the construction of the Greek language, it is possible to substitute the word "since" or "because" for the word "if." Because these four conditions are true in a believer's life, they become the fountainhead for four flowing streams of actions.

"Consolation in Christ"

The first "if" clause of Philippians 2:1 says, "If there be therefore any consolation in Christ" (KJV). Other words and thoughts that could be used for "consolation" are "encouragement," "strengthening" or "appeal." Since we are united to Christ and He has come to dwell in our lives, He is our very life and mind. Because of this there is consolation, encouragement and strengthening, as well as an appeal because of our union with Christ. This first clause in verse 1 seems to be especially associated with the command in verse 2: "Be like minded" (KJV). That is, Paul appealed to the believers in Philippi to live in total harmony with each other.

"Comfort of Love"

The second "if" clause in Philippians 2:1 says, "If any comfort of love" (KJV). Another way of saying this is: "If there is any consolation of His indwelling love," or "If there is any persuasive appeal—or power—of His love." In II Corinthians 5:14 Paul said, "The love of Christ controls us." This reveals the power there is in Christ's love, which He places within us.

This second clause of verse 1 seems to correspond with the phrase in verse 2 which says, "Having the same love" (KJV). That is, they were to have the common object of love—first a love for God and then a love for neighbors.

"Fellowship of the Spirit"

The third "if" clause in Philippians 2:1 says, "If any fellowship of the Spirit" (KJV). That is, if we have any common share in the Holy Spirit—and we do because we have trusted Christ and He indwells us.

Because of our participation in the Holy Spirit that we share, Paul said in verse 2, "Being of one accord" (KJV). We are to be united in spirit and purpose because the Holy Spirit unites; He does not divide. Our hearts are to beat in unison as we are concerned about the same things. There need be no compromise as we allow the Holy Spirit to have complete control in our lives. Inasmuch as the Holy Spirit is our one teacher, there will be oneness, or unity, as we allow Him to have control.

Compassion for Others

The fourth "if" clause of Philippians 2:1 says, "If any bowels and mercies" (KJV). Although today it is common to regard the heart as the seat of the emotions, in Bible times the bowels were considered such. Paul was here appealing to the affections that the Holy Spirit had placed within believers in regard to other believers. Having concern for others is one of the greatest indications among believers that a person is in right relationship with Jesus Christ. So in this fourth clause Paul was referring to tenderness, compassion or deep-felt affection and sympathy for others.

Because of this deep-felt affection the Holy Spirit places within us, Paul said we are to be "of one mind" (v. 2, KJV). That is, we are to be intent on one purpose; we are to have a common goal. This is what is meant by being likeminded. Before Jesus endured the death of the cross and ascended to heaven, He prayed concerning believers: "That they may all be one, even as Thou, Father, art in Me, and I in Thee, that they also may be in Us; that the world may believe that Thou didst send Me" (John 17:21). Further, Jesus prayed, "I in them, and Thou in Me, that they may be perfected in unity, that the world may know that Thou didst send Me, and didst love them, even as Thou didst love Me" (v. 23).

So it is extremely important that we believers, who are

indwelt by the Holy Spirit, be likeminded—that we have oneness of purpose. And if the mind of Christ is in us—and it is—He will unite our love, our compassion, our tenderness, our affection, our sympathy, our purpose and our intent.

Negative and Positive Exhortations

"Let nothing be done through strife or vainglory; but in lowliness of mind let each esteem other better than themselves. Look not every man on his own things, but every man also on the things of others" (Phil. 2:3,4, KJV).

Each of these verses contains both negative and positive exhortations. Paul was not just negative; he also had positive suggestions to make. Many people can be negative in their evaluation of others, but it takes insight, knowledge and wisdom to give positive suggestions.

The negative exhortation of verse 3 is: "Let nothing be done through strife or vainglory" (KJV). That is, do not be selfish; do not live just to make a good impression on others. Anything done out of selfishness or conceit is vainglory, or literally, empty glory. Those things done out of party spirit to set one faction against another is vainglory. Such things do not characterize the mind of Christ, so the believer should not have anything to do with them.

The negative exhortation of verse 4 is: "Look not every man on his own things" (KJV). That is, do not be concerned only for your personal interests. The believer is not to promote himself; this is a characteristic of the old nature, but it should not be a characteristic of the person who has the mind of Christ.

The positive exhortation of verse 3 is: "In lowliness of mind let each esteem other better than themselves" (KJV). The believer is to regard others as more important, treating them as his superiors. Paul was referring to an attitude of mind that should characterize each believer because a believer possesses the mind of Christ and this is the way Christ acted.

The positive exhortation of verse 4 is: "[Look] every man also on the things of others" (KJV). The believer should practice looking out for the interests of others. This does not mean the believer is to be unconcerned about his own affairs, but he is to be especially concerned about others even more than about himself. It does not honor the Lord for a believer to neglect himself or his affairs, but it is self-centered and uncharacteristic of the mind of Christ if the believer is concerned only about himself. When a believer loves his neighbor as himself, as the Scriptures command, he will be concerned about whatever needs his neighbor has.

"Let This Mind Be in You"

In giving exhortations to the believers in Philippi—and to all believers—Paul then made his strongest appeal: "Let this mind be in you, which was also in Christ Jesus" (Phil. 2:5, KJV). I believe that everything else in Chapter 2 revolves around this key thought. It especially emphasizes the "mind" of Christ. The Scriptures have a great deal to say about the mind, and it is a profitable study to use a concordance to find the various references and then to think carefully on each verse. Our activity really begins in the mind. If the attitude of the mind is right, a person's activities will usually be right. This is why Paul so strongly urged: "Let this mind be in you, which was also in Christ Jesus" (v. 5, KJV). This great theme of Chapter 2 relates to the sevenfold humbling of Christ, which we will discuss later.

As Paul emphasized to the Philippian believers how they should think and live, he told them they should think as Jesus Christ thought. Then Paul drove home his point by describing the kind of mind Christ had. Paul had already emphasized in Chapter 1 that Christ is our life; now he emphasized that Christ is our mind—that we are to think the way Christ thinks. Inasmuch as Christ is our life, we are to let Him have total control of our minds as well, for then even our actions will be under His control.

Seriously consider what Paul said in Romans 12:1,2: "I urge you therefore, brethren, by the mercies of God, to present your bodies a living and holy sacrifice, acceptable to God, which is your spiritual service of worship. And do not be conformed to this world, but be transformed by the renewing of your mind, that you may prove what the will of God is, that which is good and acceptable and perfect." Christ's mind is to be our mind, and we need to be transformed by the renewing of our mind.

Even though every believer actually possesses the indwelling Christ, it is possible for the believer to be working against what Christ is trying to do in his life. This is why Paul said, "Let this mind be in you, which was also in Christ Jesus" (Phil. 2:5, KJV).

The Christian life is not a stereotyped life composed of rules and regulations. It may involve rules and regulations, but the Christian life is essentially the presence of Christ in the believer. This is why Paul said, "As you therefore have received Christ Jesus the Lord, so walk in Him, having been firmly rooted and now being built up in Him and established in your faith, just as you were instructed, and overflowing with gratitude. See to it that no one takes you captive through philosophy and empty deception, according to the tradition of men, according to the elementary principles of the world, rather than according to Christ. For in Him all the fulness of Deity dwells in bodily form, and in Him you have been made complete, and He is the head over all rule and authority" (Col. 2:6-10).

It should also be remembered that the minds of different believers are not to be pressed into a single mold of thinking—this is not what is meant by being "likeminded" (Phil. 2:2, KJV). Rather, God imparts to us the matchless mastermind of Christ, so each believer will be a distinct person in himself. Believers will be likeminded inasmuch as they will seek to reach similar goals, but they will not each seek the same way, and they may not always agree as to how a particular goal can best be reached.

Because Christ is God, He has a mind that is beyond our comprehension. Yet this same Christ possesses each person who trusts Him as Saviour. Paul said, "For who has known the mind of the Lord, that he should instruct Him? But we have the mind of Christ" (I Cor. 2:16).

Consider also Romans 11:34-36: "For who has known the mind of the Lord, or who became His counselor? Or who has first given to Him that it might be paid back to him again? For from Him and through Him and to Him are all things. To Him be the glory forever. Amen."

No person can instruct the Lord; rather, it is the Lord who

instructs all believers. Inasmuch as there is one Lord instructing all believers, the result is unity when they are in His control.

We come into possession of the mind of the Lord at the time of regeneration, for at that time we become partakers of His nature. The Bible says, "For by these He has granted to us His precious and magnificent promises, in order that by them you might become partakers of the divine nature, having escaped the corruption that is in the world by lust" (II Pet. 1:4). Being partakers of His divine nature means we are also partakers of His mind—His way of thinking. And having that mind, it is important that we let Christ control us so it will be expressed through our lives.

The Christian is always to be in the process of working out the qualities of Christ's mastermind through daily living. This is what Paul had in mind when he said in Philippians 2:12: "Work out your own salvation with fear and trembling" (KJV). It is impossible to work out the characteristics of Christ's mind simply by self-effort. Each person is distinctively different and must yield himself to the control of Christ in order for the characteristics of Christ's mind to be worked out through him. We must recognize that the mind of Christ does not always express itself in the same way through each individual. Individual Christians are like separate locks which take separate keys and yet have a master key which unlocks all of them. Christ is the master key—or in this case, the mastermind—that wants to control each believer so we express His characteristics in daily living. So although each believer has his own mind, which is to be under his personal control, he also possesses the mind of Christ, and he is to allow the mind of Christ to control his life.

Things equal to the same thing are equal to each other. So when our minds are really functioning like Christ's mind, they will exhibit likeness to each other. There will be common traits among all believers when their minds are yielded to Christ, as mentioned in I John 5:1: "Whoever believes that Jesus is the Christ is born of God; and whoever loves the Father loves the child born of Him." When we trust Jesus Christ as personal Saviour and love the Father, we will discover that we will love those who have also personally trusted Christ as Saviour and love the Heavenly Father.

Three Aspects of Christ's Mind

Having told the Philippians to let the mind of Christ be in them, Paul then described three aspects of the mind of Christ. Philippians 2:6 relates to the unveiling of Christ's preexistent state—equal with the Father in all eternity. Verses 7 and 8 reveal Christ's voluntary subjection to the Father for the solution to the sin problem. Verses 9-11 tell of Christ's added glory, both now and throughout eternity, because of what He did.

Christ's Preexistent State

All of this grows out of Paul's statement: "Let this mind be in you, which was also in Christ Jesus" (Phil. 2:5, KJV). The redemption of mankind began in the mind of the Saviour because Jesus committed Himself to be the Saviour of mankind long before He became such. He is "the Lamb slain from the foundation of the world" (Rev. 13:8, KJV).

The activity of Christ is seen even in His names. Christ (which means "the Anointed One") was with the Father, but He became Jesus (which means "Saviour") because He determined in His mind to do so. He wasn't forced to do so; He made the decision out of love for fallen mankind.

As Jesus was on the earth, He continued to express this kind of thinking. The Bible says, "Just as the Son of Man did not come to be served, but to serve, and to give His life a ransom for many" (Matt. 20:28). This way of thinking that characterized Jesus Christ is also to characterize each believer. And it is in the realm of possibility because Christ indwells each believer. That is why it can be said, "We have the mind of Christ" (I Cor. 2:16).

Even though Jesus Christ indwells the believer, He does not necessarily have control of each believer's mind. This is the battle of the ages—who will control the mind? Before the fall of man, God ruled Adam and Eve through the sphere of the spirit and thus controlled each body and soul. But when Adam and Eve sinned, God moved out and their minds were left to their own control. When a person trusts Christ as

Saviour, Christ comes into his life to take up residence for the purpose of controlling the individual so that his intellect, emotions and will are what God wants them to be. Even though Christ is living within you, have you given Him full control?

Having told the Philippians to let the mind of Christ rule within them, Paul then described what Christ's attitude was: "Who, being in the form of God, thought it not robbery to be equal with God" (Phil. 2:6, KJV).

Two phrases in verse 6 show the high position that Christ has held from all eternity: "in the form of God" and "equal with God." Both of these phrases reveal the teaching of the Scriptures that Jesus Christ was—and is—God. In this high position He had glory with the Father, and when Jesus was on earth, He prayed: "Glorify Thou Me together with Thyself, Father, with the glory which I had with Thee before the world was" (John 17:5). His eternal glory preceded His humiliation. He possessed dignity and majesty, as well as the privileges and rights of deity. He possessed the fullness of all the attributes of God.

The deity of Christ is seen in the Gospel of John: "In the beginning was the Word, and the Word was with God, and the Word was God" (1:1). That the "Word" is a clear reference to Jesus Christ is evident from verse 14: "And the Word became flesh, and dwelt among us, and we beheld His glory, glory as of the only begotten from the Father, full of grace and truth."

Having established that the "Word" refers to Jesus Christ, notice what else is said of Him in this chapter: "He was in the beginning with God. All things came into being through Him; and apart from Him nothing came into being that has come into being. In Him was life; and the life was the light of men" (vv. 2-4). Concerning Jesus Christ, Colossians says, "And He is the image of the invisible God, the first-born of all creation. For in Him all things were created, both in the heavens and on earth, visible and invisible, whether thrones or dominions or rulers or authorities—all things have been created through Him and for Him. And He is before all things, and in Him all things hold together" (1:15-17). From this passage it is evident that Jesus Christ was the creator of all things.

Christ's Subjection to the Father

The decision to leave the position of glory and descend to a state of humiliation was a voluntary decision on the part of Christ—no one, not even the Father, forced Him to do so. It was in keeping with the will of the Father, but the Father did not force His Son into this situation. When He was on earth, Jesus said, "For this reason the Father loves Me, because I lay down My life that I may take it again. No one has taken it away from Me, but I lay it down on My own initiative. I have authority to lay it down, and I have authority to take it up again. This commandment I received from My Father" (John 10:17,18).

That the humiliation of Christ was voluntary is also indicated by II Corinthians 8:9: "For you know the grace of our Lord Jesus Christ, that though He was rich, yet for your sake He became poor, that you through His poverty might become rich."

These passages of Scripture reveal to us the mind of Christ—the way He thought. We are exhorted to let this same mind control our lives.

In Philippians 2:6 the word "robbery" means that Christ did not think that His position with the Father was something that should be grasped after or the act of robbery committed in order to keep. The New American Standard Bible translates this verse: "Who, although He existed in the form of God, did not regard equality with God a thing to be grasped." In other words, the Lord Jesus Christ did not insist on His own rights, but He willingly gave them up in order to come to the earth and die on the cross for your sin and mine. This is the kind of mind that we should have; this is the way we should think. Christ put us first in His thinking, and we need to put other people first in ours.

The Reason for Christ's Subjection. All of this was because Jesus Christ loved us. And His love was not simply the *phile* type of love, which is a reciprocal love, but His was an *agape* love, which is the kind that always seeks another person's highest good. And the same Jesus who had that kind of love dwells in each believer to express that love through us.

This *agape* love is described in I Corinthians 13: "Love is patient, love is kind, and is not jealous; love does not brag and is not arrogant, does not act unbecomingly; it does not seek its own, is not provoked, does not take into account a wrong suffered, does not rejoice in unrighteousness, but rejoices with the truth; bears all things, believes all things, hopes all things, endures all things" (vv. 4-7). This passage simply describes the mind of Christ, and when we are letting His mind control us, we will have the same characteristics. Then we will know experientially what is said in Romans 5:5: "The love of God has been poured out within our hearts through the Holy Spirit who was given to us."

And as we allow the Holy Spirit to pour out His love in our lives, we will then be able to effectively work out the salvation which is within us (Phil. 2:12,13). The results seen through our lives will really be the fruit of the Spirit enumerated in Galatians 5:22,23: "But the fruit of the Spirit is love, joy, peace, patience, kindness, goodness, faithfulness, gentleness, self-control; against such things there is no law."

In all of this it is important to stress again that we do not have the strength within ourselves to produce the fruit of the Spirit or the characteristics of the mind of Christ. Jesus has told us all: "Apart from Me you can do nothing" (John 15:5).

A key word in Philippians 2:6 is the one which is translated "form." The word is *morphe,* which appears three times in the New Testament and is translated "form" in each case (Mark 16:12; Phil. 2:6,7). The Greek word emphasizes the inner essence of a person or thing. Thus, Paul was telling the Philippians that when Jesus Christ was with the Father before He came to earth, He had the inner essence of God. Paul would never have consented to any teaching that made Jesus Christ less than God. Many in Paul's day (and many today) did not believe that Jesus Christ was God. Jesus Christ was not only God before He came to earth, but even while He was on earth He claimed that He was equal with God. If He had claimed to be less than God, He would not have so disturbed the leaders of the Jews. But they clearly understood what His claims were. John 5:18 says, "Therefore the Jews sought the more to kill him, because he not only had broken the sabbath, but said also that God was his Father, making himself equal with God" (KJV). Even though some today refuse to believe that Jesus Christ is God and that He is equal with the Father, the Jewish leaders clearly understood His claims, and this is why they hated Him so bitterly.

From Philippians 2:6 it is apparent that there was some element of Jesus' equality with God that He was willing to set aside during His earthly ministry. One cannot give up the qualities of his inner nature, but he can relinquish the right, in some respects, to outwardly express his inner nature. Even though Christ was God Himself and had the right to display His attributes, He willingly gave up this right in order to come to earth to be the Saviour of the world. He did not cease being in the form of God as to His inner nature, but He gave up being equal with God as far as the expression of some of His attributes was concerned.

Remember that the Father did not humble Jesus Christ; He humbled Himself. There is a vast difference between being humiliated and willingly humbling oneself. Jesus Christ voluntarily took a lower position because of His love for us. And this is the same kind of attitude that should characterize those of us who know Jesus Christ as Saviour.

The Bible has much to say about both pride and humility. James 4:6,10 says, "But He gives a greater grace. Therefore it says, 'God is opposed to the proud, but gives grace to the humble.' . . . Humble yourselves in the presence of the Lord, and He will exalt you." First Peter 5:6 says, "Humble yourselves, therefore, under the mighty hand of God, that He may exalt you at the proper time." Matthew 23:12 says, "Whoever exalts himself shall be humbled; and whoever humbles himself shall be exalted."

The Extent of Christ's Subjection. Philippians 2:7,8 tells of the extent to which the Lord Jesus Christ willingly humbled Himself. Instead of holding on to the glory He had with the Father, He "made himself of no reputation, and took upon him the form of a servant, and was made in the likeness of men: and being found in fashion as a man, he humbled himself, and became obedient unto death, even the death of the cross" (KJV).

Although there are many aspects of the humbling to which Jesus willingly subjected Himself, there are primarily two areas: the humbling involved in the act of becoming a man and the humbling that took place after He became a man.

The phrase "made himself of no reputation" (v. 7, KJV) is literally "he emptied himself." The emptying of Himself was the opposite of grasping after what He had in the presence of the Father—independent exercise of authority and the free expression of His attributes.

Instead, He "took upon him the form of a servant" (v. 7, KJV). What a difference! He became a servant in the universe in which He was really the sovereign. He had created the universe, and it was controlled by Him, yet He came to be a servant in it. There is a sense in which the angelic beings are servants of God, but Jesus humbled Himself far lower than the angels. Hebrews 2:9 says, "But we do see Him who has been made for a little while lower than the angels, namely, Jesus."

Jesus was not born into the level of life that some servants who work in wealthy households enjoy. He humbled Himself far lower than that; He was born in a stable and lived with a family of very little means.

In the phrase "took upon him the form of a servant" (v. 7, KJV), the word translated "form" is *morphe*, which is the same word translated "form" in verse 6. As to His inner essence, He was God, but when He chose to come to earth, He also took on the inner essence of a servant. The word Paul used for "servant" was the common word used in New Testament times for "slave."

What a contrast! Jesus Christ gave up the highest glory imaginable—a position of complete independence—and took the lowest position thinkable. A servant has no glory, majesty or even privileges. Rather, he has duties and obligations. A servant is not honored and served; he is to honor and to serve others.

Jesus knew well the life of a servant. On one occasion He told His listeners: "But which of you, having a slave plowing or tending sheep, will say to him when he has come in from the field, 'Come immediately and sit down to eat'? But will he not say to him, 'Prepare something for me to eat, and properly clothe yourself and serve me until I have eaten and drunk; and afterward you will eat and drink'? He does not thank the slave because he did the things which were commanded, does he? So you too, when you do all the things which are commanded you, say, 'We are unworthy slaves; we have done only that which we ought to have done' " (Luke 17:7-10).

Jesus knew that a slave's primary responsibility was to perform duties and was not to expect to receive thanks for doing so, yet this is the very level to which He subjected Himself.

Jesus often spoke of Himself as doing only that which was commanded Him by the Father. This further emphasized His role of a servant. It was well understood in the mind of Jesus that "the Son of Man did not come to be served, but to serve, and to give His life a ransom for many" (Matt. 20:28).

The mind of Christ—the manner of His thinking—was prophesied in the Old Testament. Psalm 40:7,8 says, "Behold, I come; in the scroll of the book it is written of me; I delight to do Thy will, O my God; Thy Law is within my heart." This Messianic psalm is particularly applied to Christ as it is quoted in Hebrews 10:7. Jesus' greatest desire was to do the will of the Father. And this is to be our way of thinking also. This is why Paul said, "Let this mind be in you, which was also in Christ Jesus" (Phil. 2:5, KJV).

God's way to greatness is to become a servant. Matthew 20:26,27 says, "Whoever wishes to become great among you shall be your servant, and whoever wishes to be first among you shall be your slave." As far as God is concerned, this is the road to greatness.

The Humility of Christ's Subjection. Philippians 2:7 also says of Jesus Christ that He "was made in the likeness of men" (KJV). This conveys the full reality of His human nature. He who said, "Let Us make man in Our image, according to Our likeness" (Gen. 1:26) was Himself made in man's likeness. "The Word became flesh, and dwelt among us" (John 1:14). "For what the Law could not do, weak as it was through the flesh, God did: sending His own Son in the likeness of sinful flesh and as an offering for sin, He condemned sin in the flesh" (Rom. 8:3).

To be our Redeemer, it was necessary for Jesus Christ to take upon Himself human form. "Since then the children share in flesh and blood, He Himself likewise also partook of the same, that through death He might render powerless him who had the power of death, that is, the devil" (Heb. 2:14). Jesus Christ came to be our Kinsman-Redeemer, which means He had to be like us—with the exception of sin—to redeem us.

That He had no sin is evident from many Scriptures, such as II Corinthians 5:21: "He made Him who knew no sin to be sin on our behalf, that we might become the righteousness of God in Him." With our finite minds it is hard to grasp the concept that God Himself took on human form, that He who made us in His likeness came to be made in our likeness.

Philippians 2:8 says, "And being found in fashion as a man, he humbled himself, and became obedient unto death, even the death of the cross" (KJV). Not only did Jesus willingly humble Himself in order to become man, but after becoming a man, He further humbled Himself. He was not born in a king's palace, or even in comfort, but in a cold and lonely stable. He might have been born in a mansion, but He really had no place to lay His head. His was a life of aloneness and misunderstanding. He was lied about and hunted as a criminal. He was continuously taunted by the religious leaders of His day.

But as if this were not enough, He further humbled Himself by becoming "obedient unto death, even the death of the cross" (v. 8, KJV). Through Adam's disobedience, death had come to the human race (see Rom. 5:12), but by the obedience of Jesus Christ unto death, He brought life—eternal life—to the human race (see v. 19). If the first man had obeyed, it would have meant life, but this Man (Christ) obeyed even to the point of death to bring those who believe in Him out of death into life. Jesus said, "He who hears My word, and believes Him who sent Me, has eternal life, and does not come into judgment, but has passed out of death into life" (John 5:24).

He could have died a normal death surrounded by loved ones helping Him through the dark hour, but in the one final step of His humbling, He died as only the very worst criminals did—by crucifixion. Here we are given tremendous insight into the mind of Christ. The death on a Roman cross was the most humiliating experience possible, but He was willing to undergo that because of His love for you and me. Because He sought our highest good, He gave up His glory with the Father to take upon Himself the form of a man so He could die the worst possible death and pay the penalty for sin.

Death by crucifixion was invented by the Romans for the execution of the most despicable criminals. No Roman citizen could be crucified, and only non-Romans who had committed the grossest of crimes were sentenced to this awful form of death.

The Bible says that a person who hangs on a tree is cursed: "Christ redeemed us from the curse of the Law, having become a curse for us—for it is written, 'Cursed is everyone who hangs on a tree' " (Gal. 3:13). This quotation is taken from Deuteronomy 21:22,23: "And if a man has committed a sin worthy of death, and he is put to death, and you hang him on a tree, his corpse shall not hang all night on the tree, but you shall surely bury him on the same day (for he who is hanged is accursed of God), so that you do not defile your land which the Lord your God gives you as an inheritance."

Only the mind of Christ could have compelled a person to go to such depths for others. It is the mind of lowliness, of pure and absolute love. On the cross, He gave Himself *for* us, but now He gives Himself *to* us, for we as believers possess His mind, and we are to let Him have control of our lives.

Christ's Exaltation

Philippians 2:9-11 says, "Wherefore God also hath highly exalted him, and given him a name which is above every name: that at the name of Jesus every knee should bow, of things in heaven, and things in earth, and things under the earth; and that every tongue should confess that Jesus Christ is Lord, to the glory of God the Father" (KJV).

The voluntary humbling of the Lord Jesus Christ is followed by His exaltation. His humiliation went to a greater extent than anyone could ever conceive—from God to a servant to a man to death—even to a death on the cross. But His exaltation is also more than anyone can conceive. In a sense, one might even say that it goes in the opposite direction even further than His humiliation went, if this is possible.

The word "wherefore" (v. 9, KJV) reflects on the justice of God in response to Christ's obedience and self-abasement. It is a characteristic of God that He is always just. This is true in the way He treats believers today as well as what He did for Christ. If we humble ourselves, we can rely on the fact that God is just and will exalt us in due time.

Christ's confidence in His Father was revealed as He spoke to His Father, as recorded in John 17: "I glorified Thee on the earth, having accomplished the work which Thou hast given Me to do. And now, glorify Thou Me together with Thyself, Father, with the glory which I ever had with Thee before the world was" (vv. 4,5). These words were spoken just before His final step of humiliation had been accomplished.

In Philippians 2:5-8 Jesus Christ is the one being spoken of, but verses 9-11 speak of the Father's rewarding Christ for willingly humbling Himself. The Father did not humble Christ; Christ humbled Himself. But Christ did not exalt Himself, the Father did. This is the manner of thinking of the mind of Christ—He humbles Himself, but He does not exalt Himself.

It is important for us believers to realize also that God is the one who exalts us, not we ourselves. James 4:10 says, "Humble yourselves in the presence of the Lord, and He will exalt you." The exalting must be God's work, not ours. Our responsibility is to willingly humble ourselves, even as the Lord Jesus Christ did.

Christ's Past Exaltation. The Father's rewarding for the Son's voluntary obedience is seen in three stages: First is what God has done in the past—"God also hath highly exalted him" (Phil. 2:9, KJV). At the time Paul was writing to the Philippians, he could speak of this exaltation as having taken place in the past. Christ was resurrected and brought into the presence of the Father.

That Christ anticipated His resurrection was prophesied by the psalmist: "For thou wilt not abandon my soul in Sheol; neither wilt Thou allow Thy Holy One to see the pit" (Ps. 16:10). In Peter's sermon on the Day of Pentecost, he said, "And God raised Him up again, putting an end to the agony of death, since it was impossible for Him to be held in its power" (Acts 2:24). So the past aspect of Christ's exaltation is that He has been raised from the dead by the power of God.

Christ's Present Exaltation. Second, there is a present aspect of Christ's exaltation—"and given him a name which is above every name" (Phil. 2:9, KJV). This aspect of Christ's exaltation has to do with His ascension. By the Father's power, Jesus ascended to sit at the Father's right hand. In Peter's message on the Day of Pentecost, he emphasized the resurrection of Jesus Christ: "This Jesus God raised up again, to which we are all witnesses. Therefore having been exalted to the right hand of God, and having received from the Father the promise of the Holy Spirit, He has poured forth this which you both see and hear" (Acts 2:32,33).

In his letter to the Ephesians, the Apostle Paul also referred to the present aspect of how the Father has exalted the Son: "Which He brought about in Christ, when He raised Him from the dead, and seated Him at His right hand in the heavenly places, far above all rule and authority and power and dominion, and every name that is named, not only in this age, but also in the one to come. And He put all things in subjection under His feet, and gave Him as head over all things to the church, which is His body, the fulness of Him who fills all in all" (1:20-23).

To sit at the right hand of God is the highest honor that can possibly be bestowed upon any person. It is this position that the Father bestowed upon Jesus Christ.

Notice especially that in Christ's present exaltation He has been given a "name" that is above all other names (Phil. 2:9). What name is being referred to? Verse 11 indicates it is the name "Lord." This is the same name used to translate the Hebrew word *yahweh,* from which we derive the name "Jehovah."

A name is the sum total of one's fame. How famous was Jesus to be? The Father gave Him the greatest name that could possibly be given to Him. On earth, His name was "Jesus," the meaning of which was explained to Joseph by an angel: "She will bear a Son; and you shall call His name Jesus, for it is He who will save His people from their sins" (Matt. 1:21). Although Jesus was known far and wide by this name, the fame attached to it was fleeting, for He was crucified. But today His name fills the heavens—it is a "name which is above every name" (Phil. 2:9, KJV).

The worthiness of Christ to bear the greatest of all names is seen from Revelation 5:9-13: "And they sang a new song, saying, 'Worthy art Thou to take the book, and to break its seals; for Thou wast slain, and didst purchase for God with Thy blood men from every tribe and tongue and people and nation. And Thou hast made them to be a kingdom and priests to our God; and they will reign upon the earth.' And I looked, and I heard the voice of many angels around the throne and the living creatures and the elders; and the number of them was myriads of myriads, and thousands of thousands, saying with a loud voice, 'Worthy is the Lamb that was slain to receive power and riches and wisdom and might and honor and glory and blessing.' And every created thing which is in heaven and on the earth and under the earth and on the sea, and all things in them, I heard saying, 'To Him who sits on the throne, and to the Lamb, be blessing and honor and glory and dominion forever and ever.' "

Of Jesus Christ, Revelation 19:6 says, "And I heard, as it were, the voice of a great multitude and as the sound of many waters and as the sound of mighty peals of thunder, saying, 'Hallelujah! For the Lord our God, the Almighty, reigns.' "

The name given to Jesus was "Lord," which—as previously mentioned—is associated with the Old Testament name *Yahweh,* which is the name "Jehovah." So sacred and full of majesty was this name that the Jews refused to pronounce it. Instead, they would substitute lesser names for God. Combinations of the names "Jehovah" and "Elohim" acknowledge God as the Almighty One who is ever-present.

A favorite passage of mine concerning the name of God is Exodus 6:3. God told Moses, "I appeared to Abraham, Isaac, and Jacob, as God Almighty, but by My name, Lord, I did not make Myself known to them." A comparison with Exodus 3:14 reveals that the significance of this name is "I Am Who I Am." The great "I Am" is the ever-present One, the One who is always there, and by this name each believer can live, walk and do His work.

Christ's Future Exaltation. Third, there is yet the future exaltation of Christ: "That at the name of Jesus every knee should bow, of things in heaven, and things in earth, and things under the earth; and that every tongue should confess that Jesus Christ is Lord, to the glory of God the Father" (Phil. 2:10,11, KJV).

For those who know Jesus Christ as Saviour, He will come in the future as Redeemer and Saviour to deliver them from this sinful, cursed world. But even those who have rejected Him will eventually have to admit that "Jesus Christ is Lord" (v. 11, KJV). Inasmuch as He is Lord, there is none above Him. There is no greater name and no greater authority. Even unbelievers will have to admit that He is sovereign. Even though unbelievers in this life despise the name of Jesus and heap ignominy upon it, they will someday have to admit that He is really Lord of all. They will have to admit that Jesus Christ is superior over everyone and everything.

That Christ will eventually be victorious over all is the theme of other Scriptures. In fact, I believe it is the emphasis of the entire Book of the Revelation. In Chapter 1, Jesus Christ is presented as He is today. Chapters 2 and 3 comprise letters addressed to the seven churches and reveal that judgment is to begin at the house of God. Chapters 4 and 5 and following, show that Christ is the One who has the right to open the books of final judgment. Chapter 19 tells of the time when He will be revealed from heaven and will come to the earth to war against the nations. Notice expecially what the Apostle John wrote as he told of this future time: "And I saw heaven opened; and behold, a white horse, and He who sat upon it is called Faithful and True; and in righteousness He judges and wages war. And His eyes are a flame of fire, and upon His head are many diadems; and He has a name written upon Him which no one knows except Himself. And He is clothed with a robe dipped in blood; and His name is called The Word of God. And the armies which are in heaven, clothed in fine linen, white and clean, were following Him on white horses. And from His mouth comes a sharp sword, so that with it He may smite the nations; and He will rule them with a rod of iron; and He treads the wine press of the fierce wrath of God, the Almighty. And on His robe and on His thigh He has a name written, King of Kings, and Lord of Lords" (vv. 11-16).

Revelation 20 tells of the thousand-year rule of Christ during which Satan is bound. Satan is loosed a little while at the end of the thousand years, and then he is cast into hell. Also cast into hell are all those whose names are not found written in the Book of Life (see vv. 11-15). However, even these unbelievers will have to admit that Jesus Christ is Lord.

Philippians 2:10 says that every knee shall bow "of things in heaven, and things in earth, and things under the earth" (KJV). "Things in heaven" refers to the innumerable angelic hosts; "things in earth" refers to every human being, saved or unsaved; "things under the earth" refers to the demon forces—even to Satan himself. Everyone is included—"every knee" shall bow (v. 10).

From this we see there are two aspects to the incomparable name of Christ. It means comfort to those who are His children; it means terror and condemnation to those who are not. Do not reject Jesus Christ as your personal Saviour. If you have not yet confessed your sinfulness to Him and placed your trust in Him as your Saviour, do so now before it is eternally too late. Every person must someday acknowledge Him as Lord, and you must choose whether you will know Him as your Saviour or as your Judge.

For those of us who have trusted Jesus Christ as Saviour, let us not allow the coldness of our hearts to rob us of the blessings God wants to be ours. Let us be sure that, in addition to His being our Saviour, we are also personally experiencing His lordship in our lives. Even we who have trusted Jesus Christ as Saviour will someday give account to Him (see Rom. 14:10; I Cor. 3:13-15; II Cor. 5:10). The purpose of believers' standing before the Judgment Seat of Christ is to be rewarded for what they have done for Him, but regrettably, some will have little reward, even though they will still have their salvation.

For unbelievers, however, it is an entirely different matter. Because they have rejected Jesus Christ, who paid the penalty for their sin, they will be cast into hell, the lake of fire (see Rev. 20:11-15). Unbelievers are now sneering at the name of Jesus and will have nothing to do with Him. In the western world, even the educational system, from kindergarten through university graduate level, endeavors to explain everything apart from the supernatural being of God. Although there are some Christian teachers in the public school system—and for this I am deeply grateful—the system itself is humanistic and even atheistic. But someday all unbelievers will have to admit that Jesus Christ is Lord. So if people do not recognize in this life that Jesus is Lord and trust Him as Saviour, they will have to admit in the life to come that He is Lord. They will not acknowledge Him as Saviour, but they will be forced to acknowledge Him as Lord. Even though it will be too late, they will admit that He was the promised Messiah who came to be the Saviour of the world and that they rejected Him.

When visiting the Holy Land, our group was standing at the Dome of the Rock, and our guide pointed to the East Gate of Jerusalem, which is now closed with stone and mortar. I shall never forget what our guide said to us: "You Protestants believe your Jesus is coming through that gate, but we Israelis believe that our Messiah is coming through that gate." How awesome it is to realize that those who refuse to claim Jesus Christ as personal Saviour now will someday be forced to recognize Him as the Saviour they rejected and as Lord of all.

Philippians 2:11 reveals that everyone will have to admit that Jesus Christ is Lord, "to the glory of God the Father" (KJV). Throughout the ages it has been God's purpose to bring glory to Himself, and even this final exaltation of Christ is for the same purpose. When He was on earth, Jesus Christ glorified the Father (see John 17:4). The purpose of redemption is to bring glory to the Father, but even those who refuse God's plan of redemption will have to confess that Jesus Christ is Lord, and this will bring glory to the Father. Even though people now ignore and defy God, this will not alter the fact that they will someday bring glory to the Father by having to admit that Jesus Christ is Lord.

Extent of Christ's Exaltation. Remember, never a man stooped so low as Jesus did. Although He was God, He gave up the manifestation of His attributes and humbled Himself to become a man. And as a man He further humbled Himself by willingly dying a death usually reserved for the most despised of criminals. The extent to which Christ humbled Himself is seen, by prophecy, in His outcry from the cross: "I am a worm, and not a man, a reproach of men, and despised by the people" (Ps. 22:6).

The extent to which He humbled Himself is unparalleled in history. It can be viewed as a man with a highly organized body and great intelligence going down, down, down—to the level of a worm which crawls at a man's feet. From God to man to worm. But all of this is past, for although the extent to which He humbled Himself has been unparalleled in history, so has the extent to which the Father has exalted Him been unparalleled. May we never forget all that He went through for us and that it was the way He thought (His mind) that caused Him to do all that He did to deliver us from condemnation and to provide all we need for a life of spiritual victory. No wonder Paul said, "Let this mind be in you, which was also in Christ Jesus" (Phil. 2:5, KJV).

Even as the Father exalted Jesus Christ after He had humbled Himself, so the Father will honor us in due time if we humble ourselves. Such honoring of believers is seen in Ephesians 2:4-7: "But God, being rich in mercy, because of His great love with which He loved us, even when we were dead in our transgressions, made us alive together with Christ (by grace you have been saved), and raised us up with Him, and seated us with Him in the heavenly places, in Christ Jesus, in order that in the ages to come He might show the surpassing riches of His grace in kindness toward us in Christ Jesus."

Think of it. If God the Father so honored His Son, who humbled Himself, will He not deal in like manner with His other sons (believers) who humble themselves? That this is the case is precisely stated in I Peter 5:5-7: "You younger men, likewise, be subject to your elders; and all of you, clothe yourselves with humility toward one another, for God is opposed to the proud, but gives grace to the humble. Humble yourselves, therefore, under the mighty hand of God, that He may exalt you at the proper time, casting all your anxiety upon Him, because He cares for you."

Many songs have been written through the years to emphasize the importance of Jesus' name. Many of these songs have become common to all believers, but there is a poem which is probably not well known to most Christians. It is a poem written by a converted atheist, and it expresses his thoughts as he reflected on the name of Jesus Christ.

> I've tried in vain a thousand ways
> My fears to quell, my hopes to raise;
> But what I need, the Bible says,
> Is ever, only Jesus.

My soul is night, my heart is steel—
I cannot see, I cannot feel;
For light, for life I must appeal
In simple faith to Jesus.

He died, He lives, He reigns, He pleads;
There's love in all His words and deeds;
There's all a guilty sinner needs
Forevermore in Jesus.

Tho' some should sneer, and some should blame,
I'll go with all my guilt and shame;
I'll go to Him because His name
Above all names, is Jesus.

—Jas. Procter

Chapter 4

Christ Our Mind (cont.)

"Wherefore, my beloved, as ye have always obeyed, not as in my presence only, but now much more in my absence, work out your own salvation with fear and trembling. For it is God which worketh in you both to will and to do of his good pleasure" (Phil. 2:12,13, KJV).

Work Out What God Has Worked In

Notice the command: "Work out your own salvation with fear and trembling" (Phil. 2:12, KJV). Paul commanded that we should let the mind of Christ be in us, but he did not say that this is accomplished by imitation; rather, it is accomplished by implantation. Only as we permit God to work in us (v. 13) can we work out through our lives what has been implanted there. To endeavor to imitate Christ would be only an artificial expression at best and not a genuine one. God first implants Christ's life in us so He will be at work to produce His life through us. This is God's method.

Verses 12,13 should not be interpreted to mean that one has to work *in order to* obtain salvation. Paul was writing to people who were already saved and was instructing them to express this inner salvation through their lives to others. Salvation is not a work of man for God; it is a work of God for man. The Scriptures are clear that one does not obtain salvation by works: "For by grace you have been saved through faith; and that not of yourselves, it is the gift of God; not as a result of works, that no one should boast" (Eph. 2:8,9). The purpose of good works is to express the salvation already possessed, and that is the emphasis of the following verse in

Ephesians 2: "For we are His workmanship, created in Christ Jesus for good works, which God prepared beforehand, that we should walk in them" (v. 10).

So it must be remembered concerning Philippians 2:12,13 that Paul was writing to those who have already trusted Jesus Christ as Saviour. He had emphasized that Christ is to be everything to the believer, and then he continued that thought by emphasizing how the believer is to express his salvation to others. Inasmuch as Christ is within the believer, He will—by the Holy Spirit—produce His life in the believer. As a result, the characteristics of Christ's life will be seen through the believer as he works out the salvation that is already within him. And Christ will work in us in the same proportion that we allow Him to do so.

Some basic steps in the Christian life can be appropriated simply by recognizing two of the "lets" in Scripture. First, Romans 6:12 says, "Let not sin therefore reign in your mortal body, that ye should obey it in the lusts thereof" (KJV). God has made the provision so that the believer does not have to sin; therefore, it is possible for the believer to overcome sin. Second, Philippians 2:5 says, "Let this mind be in you, which was also in Christ Jesus" (KJV). Inasmuch as the believer is indwelt by Christ, the believer is exhorted to let the same mind be in him that was in Christ—to think in the same way.

Some have said that the thought of working out what God has worked in is a mere play on words. However, I am convinced it is a basic truth of Philippians 2:12,13. To "work out" is to carry out to the goal; that is, to carry out to its ultimate conclusion. What is the goal? It is that we might be conformed to the image of Jesus Christ (see Rom. 8:28,29). And this is possible only as we appropriate the mind of Christ by letting Him control our lives.

In Philippians, Paul was not writing of justification but of sanctification. Romans 3—5 tells how justification is obtained—through faith in Jesus Christ, who has become the satisfaction for our sins. In Philippians, Paul wrote of how we become further set apart to God from sin; that is, how we have victory over self and over sin. This is also what Romans 6 is about. Paul's concern for the Christian was that he keep on making progress by working out the salvation that has already been worked in him.

"With Fear and Trembling"

Notice that Philippians 2:12 refers to working out one's salvation "with fear and trembling" (KJV). This does not refer to a slavish fear, or awesome dread, because this kind of fear does not originate with God. Romans 8:15 says, "For you have not received a spirit of slavery leading to fear again, but you have received a spirit of adoption as sons by which we cry out, 'Abba! Father!' " As a child cries out "Daddy!" when he has a special need, so God wants us to cry out to Him as our Heavenly Father.

So the fear and trembling of Philippians 2:12 refers to a wholesome caution so that with reverence, awe and self-distrust we live out the salvation that is within us. When we consider the immense sacrifice Christ made for us, we should have a grave concern that we be able to sufficiently express to others our love and appreciation for what Christ has done. This is expressed not only by our words but also especially by our lives. We want others to know that we are serious about spiritual matters. That we are not to treat our salvation lightly is also seen from Hebrews 2:3: "How shall we escape if we neglect so great a salvation?" I do not believe that the writer of Hebrews was talking to unsaved people at this point. He was referring to the great salvation we have in Jesus Christ and was pointing out what an utter shame it would be for any believer to neglect the salvation he has.

So every Christian needs to work out his salvation with a tender conscience and a watchfulness against temptations, trials or testings, shrinking from whatever might offend God or discredit His name. Paul's own testimony in this regard is seen in Acts 24:16: "In view of this, I also do my best to maintain always a blameless conscience both before God and before men." Might we have the same attitude that Paul had.

Each of us needs to seriously consider whether or not there is something in our lives that is discrediting the name and Person of Christ. When we realize what He has done for us, we ought to tremble as we stand in the presence of a holy, righteous, almighty God. Not only do we stand in His presence now, but we will also stand in His presence when we give account at the Judgment Seat of Christ. When others view our lives today, what do they see? What do they talk about? We should be constantly apprehensive of the deceitfulness of the flesh. Jeremiah 17:9,10 says, "The heart is more deceitful than all else and is desperately sick; who can understand it? I, the Lord, search the heart, I test the mind, even to give to each man according to his ways, according to the results of his deeds." We need to develop a watchfulness in regard to the power in our corruption.

Arthur S. Way paraphrases Philippians 2:12,13 this way: "Work out, with fear and self-distrust, ay, with trembling self-distrust, your own salvation. You have not to do it in your unaided strength: it is God who is all the while supplying the impulse, giving you the power to resolve, the strength to perform, the execution of His good-pleasure" (*The Letters of St. Paul,* p. 141).

Verse 13 explains how it is possible to do what is said in verse 12: "For it is God which worketh in you both to will and to do of his good pleasure" (KJV). None of this is to be done in our own strength, for it is God who is effectually working in us to energize and create within us the will and the power to do the work.

The word "will" refers to God's making us desirous to do His will. The words "worketh" and "do" are both translations of a Greek word from which we derive the word "energize."

So God the Holy Spirit is making the saint willing and desirous of doing God's sweet will, and He also provides the power to do it.

A Perfect Balance

In all of this a perfect balance is kept—God gives the divine enablement; we provide the human responsibility. We are not to be totally passive, for after God works in us, we are to work it out through our lives.

It is wonderful that we have God's help available not only to cause us to be willing to do His will but also to give us the power to perform it. So when we say, "Lord, I need Your help," God gives us the strength we need. As we grow in the knowledge of Him and mature spiritually, God aids our strength by His. But when we know Him as the indwelling

Christ—as our very life—then He upholds us and accomplishes His work in and through us. So the more we see of His strength, the less we see of our own. This is what Paul came to realize when God refused to remove the thorn from his flesh: "My [God's] grace is sufficient for you, for power is perfected in weakness" (II Cor. 12:9). When Paul understood this concept of God's enabling power, he responded: "Most gladly, therefore, I will rather boast about my weaknesses, that the power of Christ may dwell in me. Therefore I am well content with weaknesses, with insults, with distresses, with persecutions, with difficulties, for Christ's sake; for when I am weak, then I am strong" (vv. 9,10).

Regardless of where you are in your Christian life, you can expect help from God for whatever situations you face. You do not need to rise to the level of some other Christian before God will help you. He supplies whatever you need at every stage of your spiritual life.

Philippians 2:12 emphasizes the human responsibility: "Work out your own salvation" (KJV). Verse 13 emphasizes the divine enablement: "For it is God which worketh in you" (KJV). These verses reveal the perfect balance that is to be kept between God and the believer. Notice it says that God works "in" you, not "instead of" you.

Some believers become so passive in their relationship with Christ they think they are to do nothing. Some even say, "Let go and let God." However, I believe it is far more scriptural to say, "Take hold with God." God does not work instead of you; He works in you. The believer needs to see what God is doing in his life and then, by faith, live accordingly. In this way he is appropriating, or taking hold of, what God has for him.

If one really believes that the Christian has no responsibility in this relationship, he would also believe the Christian never has to say no to anything. But the Scriptures emphasize that there are many things to which the believer must say no. For instance, Romans 6:12 says, "Do not let sin reign in your mortal body that you should obey its lusts." This involves saying no to sin and its desires.

Instead of yielding to sin, believers are to "present [themselves] to God as those alive from the dead, and [their] members as instruments of righteousness to God" (v. 13). So the believer is to say no to sin and yes to God.

In the Christian life there must be a positive interaction between the free will of man and the sovereign grace of God. This fact can be illustrated by the type of power steering in an automobile which is energized only after a certain amount of pressure is applied to the steering wheel. It takes only the strength of your little finger to give the steering wheel the impulse it needs to cause the power steering to be energized. So in the Christian life, God will not act unless we first respond, but we can be sure that when we do respond, He will act in our behalf.

Response Toward God and Man

As Paul wrote to the Philippian believers, he gave them a further practical exhortation: "Do all things without murmurings and disputings: that ye may be blameless and harmless, the sons of God, without rebuke, in the midst of a crooked and perverse nation, among whom ye shine as lights in the world" (Phil. 2:14,15, KJV).

Paul's exhortation involved a response toward God and toward man. Toward God, they were to do things without murmuring and were to be blameless, sons of God, without blemish, without disputings, without fault-finding and without complaining. All of these actions and characteristics could be directed against God as a carnal believer questioned the goodness of God in his situation.

The Bible gives many warnings about murmuring against God. As Paul wrote to warn believers about this matter, he reminded them of the Old Testament Israelites: "Nor let us try the Lord, as some of them did, and were destroyed by the serpents. Nor grumble, as some of them did, and were destroyed by the destroyer. Now these things happened to them as an example, and they were written for our instruction, upon whom the ends of the ages have come" (I Cor. 10:9-11).

In his Epistle to the Philippians, Paul not only instructed them concerning their attitudes toward God, but he also instructed them concerning their attitudes toward man.

Paul said they were to be without disputings and harmless. In the world, they were to be as shining lights (2:14,15).

Paul further enjoined the Philippian believers: "Holding forth the word of life; that I may rejoice in the day of Christ, that I have not run in vain, neither laboured in vain" (v. 16, KJV).

The Greek word translated "holding forth" is in a form which indicates the action is to go on at the same time as the proper attitudes of verses 14,15. So the sense is, "While holding forth the word of life."

This shows the centrality of the Word of God to the believer's witness. The Christian is to study the Word, apply it to himself and then translate it into daily living before a crooked and perverse world. And every believer may be assured that as God's Word is held forth it will have an effect on those who hear it. Hebrews 4:12 says, "For the word of God is living and active and sharper than any two-edged sword, and piercing as far as the division of soul and spirit, of both joints and marrow, and able to judge the thoughts and intentions of the heart."

There is no substitute for holding forth God's Word, for if people are to come into right relationship with Jesus Christ, they must know what God's Word says. Romans 10:17 says, "Faith comes from hearing, and hearing by the word of Christ." So if those we witness to are to be able to have faith in Christ, they must have the Word of God presented to them.

We must first benefit from the Word ourselves before we become concerned about passing it on to others. We cannot do the work of God or have the right attitudes (as urged in the previous verses) unless God's Word is doing its work within us. The Word of God goes to the deepest parts of our nature. It exposes, sifts, analyzes and judges even our thoughts (see Heb. 4:12).

All that the Word of God accomplishes is clearly stated in II Timothy 3:16: "All Scripture is inspired by God and profitable for teaching, for reproof, for correction, for training in righteousness." The word translated "inspired" literally means "God-breathed." Inasmuch as the Word originated with God, it is profitable for the uses mentioned in verse 16, and it effectively accomplishes God's purpose in each regard.

The Word of God is profitable for teaching, reproof, correction and spiritual training. So whether we are explaining to someone his need to be born again or rebuking and correcting because of error or instructing in spiritual growth, the Word of God must be central in all that we have to say.

The purpose of all this is found in the following verse: "That the man of God may be adequate, equipped for every good work" (v. 17).

No wonder that God, through Paul, instructed Timothy: "Preach the word; be ready in season and out of season; reprove, rebuke, exhort, with great patience and instruction" (4:2).

I especially like the way the Amplified Bible renders II Timothy 3:16,17;4:2: "Every Scripture is God-breathed— given by His inspiration—and profitable for instruction, for reproof and conviction of sin, for correction of error and discipline in obedience, and for training in righteousness [that is, in holy living, in conformity to God's will in thought, purpose and action], so that the man of God may be complete and proficient, well-fitted and thoroughly equipped for every good work. . . .Herald and preach the Word! Keep your sense of urgency (stand by, be at hand and ready, whether the opportunity seems to be favorable or unfavorable, whether it is convenient or inconvenient, whether it be welcome or unwelcome, you as preacher of the Word are to show people in what way their lives are wrong) and convince them, rebuking and correcting, warning and urging and encouraging them, being unflagging and inexhaustible in patience and teaching."

Paul was especially concerned that the Philippian believers be holding forth the word of life so "that I may rejoice in the day of Christ, that I have not run in vain, neither laboured in vain" (Phil. 2:16, KJV).

Paul's concern was that, on the day when all believers give an account to Jesus Christ for the way they have served Him in this life, the believers from Philippi would receive rewards. This would be proof to Paul that his ministry with them had not been in vain, or empty. The veteran apostle was very concerned for those he had discipled in the faith. For them to be radiant witnesses while holding forth the word of life would cause him to rejoice in the day when every believer gives account to the Lord Jesus.

But if one expects rewards, he must count the cost and discipline himself to lay aside those things that do not contribute to his gaining the rewards. Concerning Moses, Hebrews 11:26,27 says, "Considering the reproach of Christ greater riches than the treasures of Egypt; for he was looking to the reward. By faith he left Egypt, not fearing the wrath of the king; for he endured, as seeing Him who is unseen."

Just as one who begins his own business expects to have rewards from it, so Paul expected a reward himself for what had been accomplished through him in the lives of the Philippian believers. Paul knew that God alone keeps the books, so only He would know what rewards to give.

Good Examples

The last segment of Philippians 2 touches on various subjects. Verses 17 and 18 tell of Paul's and the Philippians' mutual joy: "Yea, and if I be offered upon the sacrifice and service of your faith, I joy, and rejoice with you all. For the same cause also do ye joy, and rejoice with me" (KJV).

Paul was especially concerned to learn how the Philippians were faring so he told them of his intent to send Timothy for this purpose (vv. 19-23). Paul spoke highly of Timothy as he gave his reason for sending him to the Philippians: "For I have no man likeminded, who will naturally care for your state. For all seek their own, not the things which are Jesus Christ's" (vv. 20,21, KJV). Timothy was unselfish, whereas others were seeking to further their own interests.

Paul assured the Philippians that he himself planned to come before long to visit them: "But I trust in the Lord that I also myself shall come shortly" (v. 24, KJV).

This last segment of Philippians 2 provides examples of Christian leaders, and one that Paul especially singled out was Epaphroditus (vv. 25-30). Epaphroditus is mentioned by name only twice in Philippians (2:25; 4:18). In the last reference at the end of his letter, Paul said, "But I have all, and abound: I am full, having received of Epaphroditus the things which were sent from you, an odour of a sweet smell, a sacrifice acceptable, wellpleasing to God" (KJV). This reveals that the Philippians had earlier sent Epaphroditus to Rome, bearing gifts for Paul from the church. No doubt the church at Philippi intended for Epaphroditus to be whatever help he could be to the apostle during Paul's trial. But as Paul wrote to the Philippians, he said, "Yet I supposed it necessary to send to you Epaphroditus" (2:25, KJV). So although the Philippians had sent Epaphroditus to Paul, the apostle was sending him back to them.

Paul spoke highly of Epaphroditus, calling him "my brother, and companion in labour, and fellowsoldier, but your messenger" (v. 25, KJV). Paul's reason for sending Epaphroditus back to the Philippians was that "he longed after you all, and was full of heaviness, because that ye had heard that he had been sick" (v. 26, KJV). Epaphroditus must have had a very tender conscience. He was probably very sad that he was not able to be of help to Paul because of his illness, and when he heard the Philippians were concerned about his sickness, that made him feel worse.

The concern of the Philippians was justified in the case of Epaphroditus because he was ill "nigh unto death" (v. 30, KJV). Paul viewed Epaphroditus's sickness to be directly related to "the work of Christ" (v. 30, KJV). Many believers during Paul's time had suffered persecution for the cause of Christ and had earned the praise of other believers. Because of Epaphroditus's illness, Paul believed he was deserving honor in the Body of Christ. Although Paul does not give details, apparently Epaphroditus's illness was directly related to his coming to Rome to minister to Paul's needs.

Paul told the Philippians that the reason Epaphroditus had risked his life was "to supply your lack of service toward me" (v. 30, KJV). Since Epaphroditus had been sent as their representative, the intent of Paul's words seems to be that Epaphroditus did what the Philippians would have liked to have done but were unable to do. Because they could not personally come to Paul's aid, they had sent Epaphroditus as their special representative.

With these concluding remarks about Epaphroditus, Paul brought to a close this section of his letter to the Philippians which stresses the importance of having the mind of Christ and of putting others first. Paul had urged them to think in this way and then told of individuals who had done so. After referring to the Lord Jesus Christ, who gave up all for the sake of others, Paul mentioned himself, Timothy and

Epaphroditus as examples of those who put others first. Surely no one could have read the letter without getting Paul's point. And surely no believer today can read this chapter without seeing the importance of thinking as Christ thought, which results in putting others first. "Let this mind be in you, which was also in Christ Jesus" (v. 5, KJV).

Chapter 5

Christ Our Goal

In Philippians 1 we saw that Christ is our life: "For to me to live is Christ" (v. 21, KJV). In Philippians 2 we saw that Christ is our mind: "Let this mind be in you, which was also in Christ Jesus" (v. 5, KJV). If Christ is our new life and if Christ is our mind, then it follows that our innermost desires and aspirations will be to learn to know Him for who He really is to us and for us.

The key verse (really only one phrase) that summarizes that main thrust of Philippians 3 is verse 10: "That I may know him" (KJV). Paul went on to say, "And the power of his resurrection, and the fellowship of his sufferings, being made conformable unto his death" (KJV).

Warnings Against False Teachers

Verses 1-3 of Philippians 3 warn the believers against Judaizers, who were really wolves in sheep's clothing. Paul was very concerned that the Philippians be on guard concerning these false teachers. He said, "Finally, my brethren, rejoice in the Lord. To write the same things to you, to me indeed is not grievous, but for you it is safe" (v. 1, KJV).

Before Paul launched into a warning against the false teachers, he encouraged the Philippians to "rejoice in the Lord." The Greek word translated "rejoice" is used often in Philippians. It occurs in 1:18; 2:17,18,28; 3:1; 4:4,10. The King James Version translates it "rejoice" each time, with the exception of 2:17,18, where it is translated "joy." In Philippians 3:1 the word is used in a tense that emphasizes continuous rejoicing. In other words, Paul was telling the Philippians, "Keep on rejoicing in the Lord."

Notice that it is not just rejoicing, it is rejoicing "in the Lord." Everything centers in the Person of Jesus Christ as seen by the fact that Christ is our life (ch. 1) and our mind (ch. 2). Now we see that Christ is our goal (ch. 3). In order to keep on rejoicing in the Lord, it is necessary to be rooted and firmly grounded in Him so we are established in the faith (see Col. 2:6,7).

It is significant that Paul exhorted the Philippians to keep on rejoicing in the Lord before he warned them about the false teachers. It is necessary that we be firmly anchored in Jesus Christ as our foundation before we begin concentrating on related issues. The Lord Jesus Christ is the foundation who is laid in the life of every believer, and everything else of a spiritual nature must be carefully built on this foundation (see I Cor. 3:11,12).

Inasmuch as Paul was moving in Philippians 3 toward the emphasis of knowing Christ (v. 10), it was logical for him to emphasize at the beginning of the chapter one's relationship with the Lord before talking about false teachers. In a sense it is an emphasis on doctrine first and then experience. Paul wanted to be sure that the Philippians were strongly anchored in their relationship with the Lord before he began telling them about false teachers who were threatening them.

Many today are led astray by putting experience first, and they are not really grounded in the Word of God. To be grounded in the Word of God is to be grounded in the Person of Christ. As we come to know Him through the Scriptures, we will then be able to keep on rejoicing in Him. Knowing Jesus Christ to the extent that we can rejoice in Him is also a positive preventive against becoming entangled in any false teaching.

Paul told the believers in Philippi: "To write the same things to you, to me indeed is not grievous, but for you it is safe" (v. 1, KJV). To what was Paul referring by the phrase "the same things"? Perhaps it was to something already mentioned in this letter, or perhaps he was referring to other letters he had written to them since he had left Philippi. Since there seems to be little in the first part of the letter that parallels what he is about to say, he was apparently referring to warnings he had given them earlier.

To remind them of these same things, he said, was "not grievous." The word Paul used for "grievous" referred to something "troublesome." The word can also mean "lazy." Paul was emphasizing that it was not lazy of him to repeat what he had told them before, because it was evident that they needed to be warned again.

Instead of a repeated warning's being the indication of laziness, it was motivated by Paul's concern for their spiritual safety—"but for you it is safe." His warning served as a safeguard, or precaution.

The next two verses contain Paul's serious warning: "Beware of dogs, beware of evil workers, beware of the concision. For we are the circumcision, which worship God in the spirit, and rejoice in Christ Jesus, and have no confidence in the flesh" (vv. 2,3, KJV).

Paul used the word "beware" three times. The word Paul used meant to be constantly observing, to be on the alert. It has the idea of seeing an object about to fall on someone and yelling, "Watch out!" Paul saw the false teachers as serious threats to the Philippian believers, so he was urging the Philippians to watch out for the false teachers.

"Beware of Dogs"

Paul wanted the Philippian believers to watch out for "dogs" (Phil. 3:2, KJV). In the Middle East during Paul's time, dogs were normally ownerless scavengers—about as unclean an animal as one could find. The Jews had commonly referred to the religious uncleanness of the Gentiles by calling them "dogs," but Paul turned it around and used the term to refer to Jews who were confused about the gospel. They were mixing works with the gospel of grace, so although they claimed to be the clean ones, they were in reality the spiritually unclean. They were professing to be in right relationship to Christ, but their trust was not in Him alone for salvation. They had unchanged characters because they had not really come into right relationship with Jesus Christ by grace through faith. Instead, they were depending on good works as a means of salvation.

The word "dogs" is used elsewhere in the Scriptures. Revelation 22:15 says, "Outside are the dogs and the sorcerers and the immoral persons and the murderers and the idolaters, and everyone who loves and practices lying."

Paul was greatly concerned about those who were polluting the truth of the gospel with their legalistic additions. In fact, almost the entire Book of Galatians deals with this subject. And the situation has not become better with the years. In our day also we need to be aware of those who pervert the Scriptures and even put more confidence in experiences than they do in the doctrines of the Word of God.

"Beware of Evil Workers"

Paul also warned the Philippians to "beware of evil workers" (Phil. 3:2, KJV). Instead of seeing the Judaizers as doers of good that would bring glory to God, Paul viewed them as evil workers because they were reducing the Christian life to a system of dos and don'ts.

Many today are parading under the banner of Christ and yet do Him dishonor instead of honor. They use deceitful tactics to further their own cause, all the while claiming they are interested in people's spiritual welfare. This is especially true of so much of what one views and reads in the mass media. Many teach doctrines that are at great variance with the Bible and serve only to confuse those who are believers and who accept the Bible as God's Word.

The false teachers of Paul's day—as well as ours—are those who, with skill and craft, veneer error with the similitude of truth. What they have to offer is like sugar-coated pills, but their teachings have detrimental, eternal consequences. Just because there is some truth in what these religious professionals have to say does not excuse their enormous responsibility for the errors they propagate. Watch the cults and the various "isms" of our day. They are making inroads even in some evangelical circles. The best way to prevent this is by the diligent, constant proclaiming of the Word of God. When Bible truth is known, it is far easier to detect error.

"Beware of the Concision"

Paul also warned the Philippians to "beware of the concision" (Phil. 3:2, KJV). The word translated "concision" means "mutilation." The Jews were concerned about circumcision because this was a sign of God's covenant with Abraham (see Gen. 17:11). Many of the Jews during Paul's day had trusted Jesus Christ as Saviour, but some were confusing the gospel of grace by teaching that circumcision was also required for salvation. Paul viewed circumcision as simply mutilation if it were taught as being essential to salvation.

We have many parallels to this today. There are those who, contrary to the Scriptures, add various rituals as requirements for salvation. For instance, some say a person must be baptized with water before he can be saved. Such a belief is a direct reproach to the sufficiency of Christ's death on the cross to pay the penalty for sin. Nothing needs to be added to what He has accomplished; we simply come by faith and receive all that He has done for us. Baptism follows as a testimony of true intent but is not a means of salvation.

Paul told the Philippians, "For we are the circumcision" (v. 3, KJV). Since Paul was writing to Gentiles, he was not referring to physical circumcision but to a spiritual circumcision. Even in Old Testament times, physical circumcision was intended to point to the circumcision of the heart. Moses told the Israelites, "Moreover the Lord your God will circumcise your heart and the heart of your descendants, to love the Lord your God with all your heart and with all your soul, in order that you may live" (Deut. 30:6).

Circumcision is no longer required as an outward form prescribed by the Law but is an inner experience of the heart. Instead of a cutting of the flesh, it is a cutting away of the sinful things in our lives so we may honor Jesus Christ even more. This is known as true repentance.

Three Essentials of True Christianity

Having said, "We are the circumcision" (Phil. 3:3, KJV), Paul then presented three essentials of true Christianity as he described those who are the true circumcision.

"Worship God in the Spirit"

First, Paul said that true believers "worship God in the spirit" (Phil. 3:3, KJV). The word translated "in" can also be translated "by." Those who truly know Jesus Christ as Saviour worship Him by the Holy Spirit, who indwells them. As we allow the Holy Spirit to work in our lives, He will draw attention to Jesus Christ.

When Jesus was speaking to the woman at the well, He sought to clarify her concept of thinking that one must worship in a given locality. Jesus told her: "An hour is coming, and now is, when the true worshipers shall worship the Father in spirit and in truth; for such people the Father seeks to be His worshipers. God is spirit; and those who worship Him must worship in spirit and truth" (John 4:23,24).

At the time of salvation, the Holy Spirit takes up residence in the believer and makes true worship of Christ possible. That is precisely the purpose for which the Holy Spirit indwells the believer. Before Jesus left the earth, He explained what the Holy Spirit would do when He came: "He shall glorify Me; for He shall take of Mine, and shall disclose it to you" (16:14).

The spiritual enabling that the Holy Spirit gives us is also seen from Romans 8:26,27: "And in the same way the Spirit also helps our weakness; for we do not know how to pray as we should, but the Spirit Himself intercedes for us with groanings too deep for words; and He who searches the hearts knows what the mind of the Spirit is, because He intercedes for the saints according to the will of God."

From this passage we see that the Holy Spirit helps us worship God by means of our prayer life. So when we refer to "worship," it is not just public worship that is referred to, it is also the life of personal communion with God. Above all, it is a spiritual relationship rather than a ceremonial one.

Many churches seem to approach God by liturgy, or ceremony, and while this in itself is not wrong, it can take the place of a personal relationship and thereby be deluding to the worshiper. God is not interested in ceremonies; He is interested in the condition of our hearts. The psalmist realized this and expressed to God, "For Thou dost not delight in sacrifice, otherwise I would give it; Thou art not pleased with burnt offering. The sacrifices of God are a broken spirit; a broken and a contrite heart, O God, Thou wilt not despise" (Ps. 51:16,17).

"Rejoice in Christ Jesus"

Paul next listed the second essential of true Christianity that was characteristic of the true circumcision: Those who have it "rejoice in Christ Jesus" (Phil. 3:3, KJV). The word translated "rejoice" is not the common one used throughout Philippians; instead, it is a word meaning "to boast." It is a glorying in Christ Jesus because all of Christianity is centralized in His Person. Not only does Jesus give life, He gives it abundantly. He said, "I came that they might have life, and might have it abundantly" (John 10:10). Also, He gives us everything we need to live a life of godliness. Second Peter 1:3 says, "Seeing that His divine power has granted to us everything pertaining to life and godliness." No wonder Paul exclaimed in Philippians 3:10: "That I may know him" (KJV).

That Jesus Christ is everything we need is especially emphasized in Colossians 2:8-10: "See to it that no one take you captive through philosophy and empty deception, according to the tradition of men, according to the elementary principles of the world, rather than according to Christ. For in Him all the fulness of Deity dwells in bodily form, and in Him you have been made complete, and He is the head over all rule and authority."

When we realize our completeness in Jesus Christ and that He is everything we need, we will certainly rejoice, or glory, in Him and in Him alone. He is the beginning and the end—and everything in between. Hebrews 12:2 says, "Fixing our eyes on Jesus, the author and perfecter of faith, who for the joy set before Him endured the cross, despising the shame, and has sat down at the right hand of the throne of God." Revelation 1:8 says, " 'I am the Alpha and the Omega,' says the Lord God, 'who is and who was and who is to come, the Almighty.' " Colossians 3:11 says, "Christ is all, and in all." A similar statement is made in Ephesians 1:23 concerning the Church: "Which is His body, the fulness of Him who fills all in all."

"No Confidence in the Flesh"

The third essential of true Christianity that Paul said was characteristic of true circumcision is that they "have no confidence in the flesh" (Phil. 3:3, KJV). The word "flesh" refers to the old nature, or old self, and is equivalent to the self-life. The total human nature is in view here. Paul said that those who are in right relationship to Jesus Christ have no confidence in the human nature because its self-efforts attain no merit before God. The true believer realizes that the flesh contributes nothing to his spirituality.

Colossians 2:11-13 says, "And in Him you were also circumcised with a circumcision made without hands, in the removal of the body of the flesh by the circumcision of Christ; having been buried with Him in baptism, in which you were also raised up with Him through faith in the working of God, who raised Him from the dead."

It is also a truth of Romans 6:4 that "we have been buried with Him through baptism into death, in order that as Christ was raised from the dead through the glory of the Father, so we too might walk in newness of life." So those who have the true circumcision—the circumcision of the heart—have received Christ's life and all He provides.

The opposite of having confidence in the flesh is having the confidence of faith. Notice carefully that it is not confidence in faith; rather, it is a confidence of faith in Jesus Christ. Each individual must choose whether or not he will have confidence in the flesh or confidence of faith in Christ.

Paul said, "For I know that nothing good dwells in me, that is, in my flesh; for the wishing is present in me, but the doing of the good is not" (Rom. 7:18). This caused Paul to exclaim: "Wretched man that I am! Who will set me free from the body of this death?" (v. 24). Paul answered his own question in the following verse: "Thanks be to God through Jesus Christ our Lord! So then, on the one hand I myself with my mind am serving the law of God, but on the other, with my flesh the law of sin" (v. 25). Paul further explained, "For the law of the Spirit of life in Christ Jesus has set you free from the law of sin and of death" (8:2).

Paul's Basis for Self-Righteousness

As Paul wrote to the Philippians, reminding them that those who are in right relationship to Christ have no confidence in the flesh, he enumerated those things of the flesh which he could have had confidence in if he had chosen to do so: "Though I might also have confidence in the flesh. If any other man thinketh that he hath whereof he might trust in the flesh, I more: circumcised the eighth day, of the stock of Israel, of the tribe of Benjamin, an Hebrew of the Hebrews; as touching the law, a Pharisee; concerning zeal, persecuting the church; touching the righteousness which is in the law, blameless" (Phil. 3:4-6, KJV).

If anyone had reason for confidence in the flesh because of natural endowments and attainments, Paul certainly could have. In fact, Paul claimed to have more reason to place confidence in the flesh than anyone else: "If any other man thinketh that he hath whereof he might trust in the flesh, I more" (v. 4, KJV).

In verses 5 and 6, Paul listed those things in which he had formerly gloried but which he renounced at his conversion in favor of knowing Jesus Christ, as the only true righteousness. These things had meant much to him, but when he came to know Christ, he renounced them as worthless rubbish. They contributed nothing toward the attainment of true life which he found in Christ.

"Circumcised the Eighth Day"

In enumerating the former things that he had gloried in, Paul listed seven specifics. First, he said he was "circumcised the eighth day" (Phil. 3:5, KJV). Paul's circumcision was in accordance with the Mosaic Law (see Lev. 12:3). Probably many of the Judaizers could not have boasted this, for some were no doubt Gentiles who had converted to Judaism and had been circumcised as adults. Paul had the heredity and the sign of the covenant. He was proud of his position as a true Israelite. It should be underscored, however, that even in Old Testament times the Jews were not saved by these outward signs; rather, they were saved by faith. Such passages as Hebrews 11:6 and Romans 4:5,9 reveal that without faith it is impossible to please God and that the Old Testament believers were saved by faith. When parents in the Old Testament had their children circumcised, it was

evidence that the parents in the Old Testament had confidence in the covenants and promises of God. The keeping of
the Law or of these various signs did not obtain salvation
but merely expressed a salvation already attained by faith
in God.

Some today mistakenly teach that if a person is born into a
Christian family, he inherits salvation from the parents. I
believe this is contrary not only to the direct teaching of the
New Testament but also to the teaching of the Old Testament. It is a uniform principle of Scripture that an individual
is saved by grace through faith. In Old Testament times
believers looked ahead to the sacrifice for sin that would end
all sacrifices, and in New Testament times and onward we
look back to what Christ has accomplished for us. But each
one is saved by faith and not by birth into a Christian family
or by works. It is said of Abraham that "being fully assured
that what He [God] had promised, He was able also to perform. Therefore also it was reckoned to him as righteousness" (Rom. 4:21,22).

Even in my own case, I had to realize that relatives who
were in right relationship to Jesus Christ had nothing to do
with my personal relationship. My grandfather and his
brother were both preachers. My father was a minister and a
missionary. But at the age of 20 I came to realize that even
though I had been born into a Christian home, I needed
Jesus Christ as my personal Saviour. At that time I became
born again, not depending on any so-called covenant or on
the salvation of other family members.

So I ask you specifically, regardless of what your relatives
possess, do you have a personal relationship with Jesus
Christ? Have you come to the realization that you are a
sinful human being and that you stand under the condemnation of sin? Do you realize that Jesus Christ has paid the
full penalty for your sin? If you will place your trust in Jesus
Christ as your personal Saviour, He will save you from your
sin and deliver you from condemnation. But if you have not
made this personal decision, in eternity to come it will not
really matter what decisions your parents and other relatives have made. Each one must give account to God.

"Of the Stock of Israel"

Second, Paul said he was "of the stock of Israel" (Phil. 3:5, KJV). In this phrase we see the pride of his birth. His parents were not proselytes; they were Hebrews by birth also. Paul was proud of his unblemished pedigree—he was a pure-blooded descendant of Abraham, not one who had been grafted in. Being of the stock of Israel meant that he had a distinguished ancestry—people like Abraham, Moses and David.

"Of the Tribe of Benjamin"

Third, Paul said he was "of the tribe of Benjamin" (Phil. 3:5, KJV). This phrase reveals that, in his unsaved state, Paul was proud of his tradition. The tribe of Benjamin gave the first king (Saul) to Israel. The tribe of Benjamin (along with Judah) remained true to God when the other ten tribes broke away from the united kingdom. Being a Benjamite was something to be proud of.

"An Hebrew of the Hebrews"

Fourth, Paul said he was "an Hebrew of the Hebrews" (Phil. 3:5, KJV). This reveals pride of prestige. In Paul's time some of the Jews had adopted the Greek language and customs and were known as the "Hellenistic Jews." However, Paul knew the Hebrew customs and spoke the Hebrew language. He was educated under Gamaliel, an outstanding Jewish educator of that day. One day when making a defense before the people of Jerusalem, Paul said, "I am a Jew, born in Tarsus of Cilicia, but brought up in this city, educated under Gamaliel, strictly according to the law of our fathers, being zealous for God, just as you all are today" (Acts 22:3).

"A Pharisee"

Fifth, Paul said that he was "as touching the law, a Pharisee" (Phil. 3:5, KJV). This was pride of orthodoxy. On one occasion Paul said, "I am a Pharisee, a son of Pharisees"

(Acts 23:6). Paul was a religious perfectionist, a Pharisee with the highest rank concerning orthodoxy and strict conformity to the requirements of the Law. In addition to the Law of Moses, the Pharisees observed many laws of tradition. In fact, it is said that the Pharisees had 365 laws that related to keeping the Sabbath.

By birth, Paul was an Israelite, and by upbringing, he was a true Hebrew. But by his own choice he was a Pharisee. The Pharisees stuck to the letter of the Law instead of to the spirit of the Law. In fact, they would even use some laws to get around others. Some today also seem to be concerned only about the letter of the law and not about the spirit of the Word of God. We need to be serious students of the Word of God, but we must make sure that it is more than just information to us. We need to respond to the information so that God's Word is translated into daily living.

Persecutor of the Church

Sixth, Paul said about himself, "Concerning zeal, persecuting the church" (Phil. 3:6, KJV). This reveals the pride of personal devotion to his religious choices. In a sense, it was Paul's pride of reputation. He was more devoted than any of his contemporaries. He was not only a Pharisee, but he was also a very zealous one. He was a conscientious and relentless persecutor of all who were considered heretics outside of his pharisaic Judaism.

Even at the time of Paul's conversion he was on his way to Damascus to persecute believers in Jesus Christ and to bring them bound to Jerusalem (Acts 9:2). "Suddenly there shined round about him a light from heaven: and he fell to the earth, and heard a voice saying unto him, Saul, Saul, why persecutest thou me? And he said, Who art thou, Lord? And the Lord said, I am Jesus whom thou persecutest: it is hard for thee to kick against the pricks" (vv. 3-5, KJV). The Holy Spirit had been bringing conviction to Paul, but he had been resisting it—he had been kicking against the pricks even as an animal kicks when goaded. But on the way to Damascus Paul came to his spiritual senses and trusted Jesus Christ as his Lord and Saviour.

Later, when writing to Timothy, Paul said of himself:

"Even though I was formerly a blasphemer and a persecutor and a violent aggressor. And yet I was shown mercy, because I acted ignorantly in unbelief" (I Tim. 1:13). In Paul's unsaved state in Judaism, he actually thought he was doing the will of God by persecuting the believers in Jesus Christ. He measured his religion by his hatred for Christians.

It is regrettable that even today some believers measure their Christian zeal by what they are against. Some have so much bitterness against modernists—those with liberal theology; others contend zealously over the issue of the Holy Spirit or over a particular translation of the Bible. Some have bitterness toward sinners, not distinguishing the sin from the sinner. But remember, a reputation of zeal against anything is not a proof of salvation in itself. I believe that when we are rightly related to Jesus Christ, we will have much zeal against those things which dishonor Him, but it is possible for people to be zealous against some things without having a right relationship with Christ.

Blameless According to the Law

Seventh, Paul said of himself: "Touching the righteousness which is in the law, blameless" (Phil. 3:6, KJV). This is a reference to pride of character, or conduct. Even in his unsaved state, no one could point a finger at Paul and say, "Look at that scoundrel!" Others had to look up to him, for he was so zealous regarding his righteousness that he was blameless. What a tremendous claim.

This indicates that Paul was a man of great stature and worth in his own eyes, as well as in the eyes of other people. In his unregenerate state, Paul's personal ego was pleased; others approved and praised him. But as Paul told about how he could glory in the things of his old life, God was not mentioned even once. Much that goes by the name of religion is only that. So often it is merely an attempt to be and to do what is considered good. It is based on a system of ethics that satisfies a human standard but utterly fails to justify a person in the sight of God. Romans 3:20 says, "By the works of the Law no flesh will be justified in His sight; for through the Law comes the knowledge of sin."

True religion relates us to God through Jesus Christ.

Christianity is a relationship to a Person. We are saved, justified and approved by Him. Approval by man is one thing, but approval by God is quite another.

When a person is born again, his life takes on a new center. It is then "For to me to live is Christ" (Phil. 1:21, KJV).

Many people think that all that is necessary to be rightly related to God is sincerity. Such a belief substitutes sincerity for knowing the truth and acting upon it. In his unsaved state, Paul was totally sincere, and no one was more zealous than he, yet he was sincerely wrong. He said, "I acted ignorantly in unbelief" (I Tim. 1:13).

Paul's sincerity, which was based on false knowledge, led him to a course of action that became a deep regret to him in later life. To the Galatians he said, "For you have heard of my former manner of life in Judaism, how I used to persecute the church of God beyond measure, and tried to destroy it; and I was advancing in Judaism beyond many of my contemporaries among my countrymen, being more extremely zealous for my ancestral traditions" (Gal. 1:13,14). To the Corinthians he said, "For I am the least of the apostles, who am not fit to be called an apostle, because I persecuted the church of God" (I Cor. 15:9). As we have already seen, he told Timothy that he thanked God for using him, "Even though I was formerly a blasphemer and a persecutor and a violent aggressor. And yet I was shown mercy, because I acted ignorantly in unbelief" (I Tim. 1:13).

But on the way to Damascus the Lord met Paul, and all this changed. Paul there realized how futile were all the things he had pride in and how helpless these virtues were in bringing him into a right relationship with God. When he saw Jesus Christ as He really is, Paul was led to making a life-changing decision. A complete change took place once for all.

Paul's Change of Values

As Paul wrote to the Philippians, he referred to his past conversion when he said, "But what things were gain to me, those I counted loss for Christ" (Phil. 3:7, KJV). The word translated "counted" means "to think" or "to consider." It is significant that Paul used this word in the Greek perfect tense, indicating a completed act with a continuing effect. At a time in the past Paul had considered all of these gains to really be losses—and he still considered them to be losses!

Paul used the same word for "count" in verse 8 as he did in verse 7. Paul said, "Yea doubtless, and I count all things but loss for the excellency of the knowledge of Christ Jesus my Lord" (KJV). However, in verse 8 Paul used a different tense to give a different emphasis. In verse 7 he used the Greek present tense to refer to a past decision that had an effect which continued right up to the present—the time when he was writing. In verse 8, he used the Greek present tense, which emphasizes continuous action in present time. In other words, he was saying, "And I am continually counting all things but loss."

When Paul wrote to the Philippians, it had been about 30 years since he had trusted Jesus Christ on the way to Damascus. At the time of his conversion, the things enumerated in Philippians 3:5,6 that were the basis of so much pride to Paul were suddenly counted as loss. And after 30 years he was still counting them as worthless in comparison to what he had found in Christ.

Notice that Paul did not count these things as loss for some other religion or creed but for Christ. In essence, Christianity is Christ. To the believer it is "not I, but Christ" (Gal. 2:20, KJV). When he was confronted by Christ on the road to Damascus, Paul asked: "Lord, what wilt thou have me to do?" (Acts 9:6, KJV). From that point forward, Christ was Paul's Lord and Master.

At first, Christ revealed Himself to Paul, as indicated in I Corinthians 15:8: "Last of all, as it were to one untimely born, He appeared to me also." At this time Christ was revealed *to* Paul, but other Scriptures tell of Christ's being revealed *in* him. Paul said, "But when He who had set me apart, even from my mother's womb, and called me through His grace, was pleased to reveal His Son in me, that I might preach Him among the Gentiles, I did not immediately consult with flesh and blood" (Gal. 1:15,16). The light that first shone *about* Paul became a transforming illumination *within* him. After that his whole life revolved around the Person of Christ.

The centrality of Christ is seen in Paul's statements con-

cerning salvation: "That if you confess with your mouth
Jesus as Lord, and believe in your heart that God raised Him
from the dead, you shall be saved; for with the heart man
believes, resulting in righteousness, and with the mouth he
confesses, resulting in salvation" (Rom. 10:9,10). Notice the
emphasis of Paul on the lordship of Christ. Some never
emphasize a turning from sin, but Paul emphasized that
Jesus Christ is to be Lord; that is, He is to be Master in our
lives.

Although some say little, if anything, about turning from
sin, the Bible says, "Unless you repent, you will all likewise
perish" (Luke 13:3). So an individual is to receive Jesus
Christ not only as his Saviour but also as his Lord, which
implies a rejection of past sins and a dependence on Christ.
We grow in our knowledge of the lordship of Christ as we
mature in the Christian life; nevertheless, at the time of
salvation there is to be an attitude of heart which says, "I am
willing to turn from my sin and to turn my life over to Jesus
Christ."

Paul's reversal of values was instant and complete: "What
things were gain to me, those I counted loss for Christ" (Phil.
3:7, KJV). Although several things are mentioned in verses 5
and 6, Paul lumped them all together in verse 7 as he used the
singular form of "loss." Actually, Paul considered these
things to be more than "loss." The Greek work Paul used had
the sense of "damage." Think of how the Judaizers would
have reacted to such a statement! What they considered to be
so significant Paul not only considered to be a loss but even a
damage in comparison to what he had in Jesus Christ.

Although verse 7 refers to the time of conversion, verse 8
reveals that Paul was still counting these things as loss 30
years later. Perhaps some of the Judaizers might have said,
"Although Paul counts them as loss now, he will change his
mind later." Paul indicated, however, that he was still counting all of these things as loss, so he had not changed his
mind about this matter during the 30 years that had elapsed.
And it could be assumed that if Paul found anything else
that resulted from the self-life he would have included it, too,
as loss.

This is the first step in any Christian's life. Once Christ
has become our life (Phil. 1:21), there has to be a definite

change, a continual turning to Him, throughout our walk in this world. Jesus said, "If anyone wishes to come after Me, let him deny himself, and take up his cross daily, and follow Me. For whoever wishes to save his life shall lose it, but whoever loses his life for My sake, he is the one who will save it" (Luke 9:23,24).

Notice again Paul's statement: "Yea doubtless, and I count all things but loss for the excellency of the knowledge of Christ Jesus my Lord" (Phil. 3:8, KJV). The Amplified Bible translates this phrase: "Yes, furthermore I count everything as loss compared to the possession of the priceless privilege—the overwhelming preciousness, the surpassing worth and supreme advantage—of knowing Christ Jesus my Lord."

This verse presents an analogy similar to bookkeeping. On the one side, all the debits, or losses, are recorded; on the other side all the credits, or gains, are recorded. Paul was saying that on the loss side of the ledger he had many things to be listed, but on the gain side only one item needed to be entered—Jesus Christ. This one item of gain more than offset all of the losses.

Concerning those things which Paul counted as loss he said, "And do count them but dung, that I may win Christ" (Phil. 3:8, KJV). Notice that the things Paul considered as dung, or refuse, were not evil things in themselves. They were not bad habits or particular sins or evil companions. They were good things, but they were not good enough to bring him into right relationship with Christ.

As someone has said, "In this sense, a good thing can become a bad thing because it becomes the substitute for the best thing." Concerning the subject we are discussing, I would change the expression to say that a good thing can become a substitute for the real thing. Paul had been following a false hope, but on the way to Damascus he had come into right relationship with Christ and now had a hope that was based on the facts.

Notice that Paul counted all these things as loss in order that he might gain Christ. There can be no spiritual gain without loss. This is a fact of life. Jesus said, "Unless a grain of wheat falls into the earth and dies, it remains by itself alone; but if it dies, it bears much fruit. He who loves his life loses it; and he who hates his life in this world shall keep it to life eternal" (John 12:24,25; see also Luke 9:23,24).

So regeneration demands renunciation. He who has not renounced anything has not gained anything. Paul let go of that which he attained by works, and he took hold of that which he had obtained by faith in Christ Jesus.

Progress in Christ

Note the progression as Paul developed the central theme of his relationship to Christ. Paul did not say that all of these changes took place immediately, but his decision to trust Jesus Christ as Saviour immediately began the process. Thus, salvation itself is a climactic decision from which many things result. At the moment of salvation one changes his mind about himself, about God and about sin. His decision to trust Jesus Christ as Saviour and Lord will later be reflected in his life-style as he turns from sin and desires more and more to please Jesus Christ in everything.

As we read Philippians 3, we see the outreach of the apostle's soul toward the great goal of every true believer—the all-absorbing quest as seen in the climaxing focal point of verse 10: "That I may know him" (KJV).

Notice some phrases in verses 8 through 12 that indicate progress. In verse 8 Paul said, "That I may win" (KJV). Paul counted as loss everything he had attained by self-effort in order that he might win, or gain, the Lord Jesus Christ by faith.

Then Paul said, "And be found in him" (v. 9, KJV). Paul did not want to be found following a law system but the Person of Jesus Christ.

In verse 10 he said, "That I may know him" (KJV). This was the focal point of Paul's life.

"[That] I might attain," he added in verse 11 (KJV). Because of Paul's relationship with Jesus Christ he wanted to go on with the Lord.

Finally, Paul said in verse 12, "That I may apprehend" (KJV). Paul realized that Jesus Christ had chosen him for a purpose, and he wanted to accomplish that purpose.

In verse 8, Paul told how he had counted all the things of the old life as loss "that I may win Christ" (KJV). He, at that time, had already been won by Christ, so Paul's salvation was not the subject here. Rather, he wanted to further gain by appropriating Christ as his complete life. He wanted the full realization of Christ living in him—and this should be the desire of every believer. If you have trusted Jesus Christ as your personal Saviour, do you also know Him as your life? Do you know Him as the One who lives in you and wants to live His life through you?

Remember, as long as the believer tries to live the Christian life in his own strength, Christ cannot work. It is either only Christ or only you; there can be no combination of the two. This does not mean that we have no responsibility; it means that we are to depend completely on Christ, not on ourselves. Our responsibility is to lay aside all the things that should not be in our lives so Christ may take complete control of us.

There should be nothing in our lives that hinders Christ from having complete access to all aspects of our lives. This is what led Paul to say, "I have been crucified with Christ; and it is no longer I who live, but Christ lives in me; and the life which I now live in the flesh I live by faith in the Son of God, who loved me, and delivered Himself up for me" (Gal. 2:20). In this regard, we have pointed out previously that Colossians 2:6 is also a key verse: "As you therefore have received Christ Jesus the Lord, so walk in Him." The believer has received Jesus Christ by faith, so he is to live by faith. The believer is to renounce all sin and to trust God for each step in his life.

The renouncing of sin is the believer's responsibility. In Romans 6, after stating that we have died with Christ and have been buried and raised with Him so we might live for Him, verse 12 says, "Therefore do not let sin reign in your mortal body that you should obey its lusts." Instead of obeying sin, the believer is to obey God and to present himself to God as one who is "alive from the dead" (v. 13). So the Christian life involves saying no to sin and yes to God. God will not force us to do this, but when we make this decision, He will give the power we need to do that which honors Him.

Colossians 1:29 tells us what Christ will do when we totally yield to Him: "For this purpose also I labor, striving

according to His power, which mightily works within me."
When we totally yield to Christ, He mightily works in us.

The Apostle Paul wanted all the blessings and the benefits
that were available in Christ. He wanted to demonstrate
what Christ could do in and through him.

One could compare Paul's significant accomplishments in
the Jewish faith with what he wanted to accomplish in the
Christian faith. It must have taken tremendous willpower to
accomplish all he did in Judaism, but he considered all that
as loss that he might cooperate with Jesus Christ in working
in and through him (see Phil. 2:12,13). Paul was persuaded
that Christ could do mighty things in and through him, and
that is why he said, "I can do all things through Christ
which strengtheneth me" (4:13, KJV).

"Be Found in Him"

As Paul wrote to the Philippians, he expressed his desire:
"And be found in him, not having mine own righteousness,
which is of the law, but that which is through the faith of
Christ, the righteousness which is of God by faith" (Phil. 3:9,
KJV). Here Paul spoke of his position in his new relationship
with Christ. This position in Christ is the foundation for all
future growth of the believer.

Notice the contrast between the two forms of righteousness referred to in verse 9. There is a righteousness which is
of the Law, and there is a righteousness which is through
faith in Christ. Paul also spoke of the righteousness of God
that comes apart from the Law in Romans 3:21,22: "But now
apart from the Law the righteousness of God has been
manifested, being witnessed by the Law and the Prophets,
even the righteousness of God through faith in Jesus Christ
for all those who believe; for there is no distinction."

In Romans 3 Paul was referring to the way a person comes
into relationship with Jesus Christ. In Philippians 3 Paul
was referring to recognizing one's position in Christ once he
has made the decision to trust Him as Saviour. This is why
he desired to "be found in him" (v. 9, KJV). Paul wanted to
demonstrate that the righteousness of Christ produced in
and through him was far superior to anything that could be
produced by self-effort under the Law system.

What Christ can accomplish for the believer is seen in the benediction of Hebrews 13. The writer asked that Jesus Christ "equip you in every good thing to do His will, working in us that which is pleasing in His sight, through Jesus Christ, to Whom be the glory forever and ever. Amen" (v. 21). Because Christ accomplishes so much more in us than the Law ever could, Paul urged the Philippians to work out the salvation that had been worked in them (see Phil. 2:12,13).

In Romans 8, Paul contrasted the works of the Spirit and the works of the Law: "For the law of the Spirit of life in Christ Jesus has set you free from the law of sin and of death. For what the Law could not do, weak as it was through the flesh, God did: sending His own Son in the likeness of sinful flesh and as an offering for sin, He condemned sin in the flesh, in order that the requirement of the Law might be fulfilled in us, who do not walk according to the flesh, but according to the Spirit" (vv. 2-4).

By the power of the Spirit, the believer is to put to death the deeds of the flesh (see v. 13). And it is possible for the believer to do this because Christ works in him to empower him to do this. Paul alluded to the power of Christ in him when he said, "To this end I labor, struggling with all the energy he so powerfully works in me" (Col. 1:29, NIV). The Amplified Bible renders this verse: "For this I labor [unto weariness], striving with all the superhuman energy which He so mightily enkindles and works within me."

Justifying righteousness cannot be seen by others because it takes place within the individual when he places his faith in Jesus Christ as his Saviour. Paul's concern in Philippians 3, however, was that he might have a personal righteousness which others could see. This personal righteousness has to be based on the one foundation, Jesus Christ. Paul said, "For no man can lay a foundation other than the one which is laid, which is Jesus Christ" (I Cor. 3:11).

Once Christ is in his life, a person has the foundation necessary to develop a personal righteousness. Paul wanted his life to demonstrate what it could not demonstrate under the Law. He wanted a personal righteousness that could be only produced by Christ in him. To accomplish this, Paul realized his knowledge of Christ needed to increase more and more. He needed more than just knowledge about Christ; he needed to know Christ intimately and experientially.

In this regard Paul was similar to Job, who lived in Old Testament times. The Book of Job gives the account of the severe testing Job went through as God and Satan struggled to have Job's allegiance. God proved He was able to hold on to Job in spite of the testings that Satan was allowed to bring into his life. The conclusion of the book records several questions God asked Job to humble him so that he was not lifted up with false pride.

When God finished with him, Job exclaimed, "I have heard of Thee by the hearing of the ear; but now my eye sees Thee; therefore I retract, and I repent in dust and ashes" (42:5,6). Even though Job was a believer before, he gained a more intimate knowledge of God because of his experiences and because God revealed more of Himself to him. And the better Job learned to know God, the more he abhorred himself because he realized how far short he came of God's glory.

Chapter 6

Christ Our Goal (cont.)

One of the most fervent desires of Paul's life was that he might know Christ.

"That I May Know Him"

In Philippians 3:10, Paul was not referring to knowing Christ as far as salvation is concerned. Paul had already trusted Jesus Christ as his personal Saviour and had been delivered from eternal condemnation. But Paul's concern as a believer was to know Christ in such a way that he might progressively become more deeply and intimately acquainted with Him. The Amplified Bible renders verse 10: "[For my determined purpose is] that I may know Him—that I may progressively become more deeply and intimately acquainted with Him, perceiving and recognizing and understanding [the wonders of His Person] more strongly and more clearly. And that I may in that same way come to know the power outflowing from His resurrection [which it exerts over believers]; and that I may so share His sufferings as to be continually transformed [in spirit into His likeness even] to His death, [in the hope]."

Romans 6:1-10 refers to the knowledge of Christ Himself, who is the supreme object of the believer's desire. It should be the goal of every believer to really know Jesus Christ—not only to know what He has done for us but also to know what He wants to accomplish in us.

In Romans 6 Paul emphasized that we are to know we have been crucified together with Him (vv. 3,6), we are to know we have been buried with Him (v. 4), we are to know we

107

have been raised with Him to new life (vv. 4,5), and we are to know Him as our life (v. 11).

Paul also told believers, "If then you have been raised up with Christ, keep seeking the things above, where Christ is, seated at the right hand of God. Set your mind on the things above, not on the things that are on earth. For you have died and your life is hidden with Christ in God. When Christ, who is our life, is revealed, then you also will be revealed with Him in glory" (Col. 3:1-4).

The difference between knowing Christ for salvation and knowing Him as one's life can be compared to a married couple. At the time of marriage, the couple may have known much about each other. This knowledge provided a basis for their marriage relationship. The knowledge at that point, however, was extremely small in comparison to what it will be after they have lived together many years and have *really* come to know each other. Whereas Paul had the basic knowledge for salvation, he wanted to go on in his Christian life to really know Christ in a personal way.

The Power of Christ's Resurrection

Paul especially wanted to know the resurrection power of Christ—"that I may know him, and the power of his resurrection" (Phil. 3:10, KJV). Paul's desires are clearly seen from this verse as rendered by the Amplified Bible: "That I may in that same way come to know the power outflowing from His resurrection [which it exerts over believers]." Paul wanted to know by experience in his daily life the same power that raised Jesus Christ from the dead. He wanted that power to be surging through his whole being, overcoming sin in his life and producing the life of righteousness and the wonderful graces mentioned in Galatians 5:22,23, which are known as the fruit of the Spirit. In writing to the Ephesians, Paul also alluded to this power of God: "And what is the surpassing greatness of His power toward us who believe. These are in accordance with the working of the strength of His might which He brought about in Christ, when He raised Him from the dead, and seated Him at His right hand in the heavenly places" (Eph. 1:19,20).

Man knows about all kinds of power, but he has never been

able to create a power that can bring a dead person back to life. That kind of power belongs to God. God displays this kind of power in the believer because Christ Himself takes up residence in the believer to live out a righteous life in him. The same power that raised Christ from the dead is exercised in the believer as Christ lives in him.

"Power" implies that which overcomes resistance. The Greek word translated "power" in Philippians 3:10 refers to power in the sense of "ability." God gives us the ability to overcome the resistance of the old nature. Paul referred to the gospel's having this kind of power when he wrote: "For I am not ashamed of the gospel, for it is the power of God for salvation to every one who believes, to the Jew first and also to the Greek" (Rom. 1:16).

It is for this power—the ability to overcome resistance—that Paul also prayed for the Ephesians (see Eph. 3:16-21). Paul was not only concerned that he himself experience the resurrection power of Christ, but he also wanted other Christians to experience this same power.

The Fellowship of Christ's Sufferings

As Paul wrote to the Philippians, he expressed his desire to also know "the fellowship of his sufferings, being made conformable unto his death" (Phil. 3:10, KJV). The Amplified Bible renders this phrase: "That I may so share His sufferings as to be continually transformed [in spirit into His likeness even] to His death, [in the hope]."

In Paul's daily life, he wanted to be transformed by the Spirit into the likeness of Jesus Christ—even that of His death. Paul was not referring to physical death but rather to death to self. Paul referred to Christ's death to self in Philippians 2:7: "But made himself of no reputation, and took upon him the form of a servant, and was made in the likeness of men" (KJV).

Paul wanted a "fellowship" (3:10), or a joint participation, in this kind of death. Paul wanted to experience a self-emptying of himself even as Jesus Christ had of Himself. This was a death to self for the sake of others. Only the indwelling, resurrected Christ can live out this kind of life—the self-abasing life—in and through the believer. Thus,

Christ's indwelling alone can conform us to the same spirit and temper of His life; that is, the meekness, lowliness and total submission that characterized Jesus Christ.

Further, Paul said, "If by any means I might attain unto the resurrection of the dead" (v. 11, KJV). The expression "if by any means" is not one of doubt but one of humility. It is a modest but assured hope. Paul, who wrote this, also wrote: "There is therefore now no condemnation for those who are in Christ Jesus" (Rom. 8:1). He also wrote that nothing "shall be able to separate us from the love of God, which is in Christ Jesus our Lord" (v. 39).

So in Philippians 3:11, Paul was not doubting his salvation but was only concerned that he might attain a certain goal related to the resurrection power of the Lord Jesus Christ. The "resurrection of the dead" (v. 11, KJV) is literally a "resurrection out from among the dead" or an "out resurrection from the dead."

Paul spoke much of the physical resurrection that awaits each person in the future, but in Philippians 3 he was concerned about living the resurrected power of Christ in his daily life. Although living among the spiritually dead, he wanted to know Christ intimately so he could live among the spiritually dead as one in whom Christ was very much alive. Paul wanted his life not only to fully demonstrate what Christ had done for him but also to demonstrate what Christ could do in his life.

Eagerly Pressing Toward the Goal

Verses 12-14 of Philippians 3 tell of Paul's eagerly pressing toward the goal of being Christlike. It should be the object, or goal, of every believer to be Christlike. God wants to conform us into the image of His Son (see Rom. 8:29). We are assured that eventually we will be completely like Christ: "Beloved, now we are children of God, and it has not appeared as yet what we shall be. We know that, when He appears, we shall be like Him, because we shall see Him just as He is" (I John 3:2). Just knowing that eventually we will be like Christ will have an effect on our lives: "Every man that hath this hope in him purifieth himself, even as he is pure" (v. 3, KJV).

Even though we are in the process of being like Christ now,

we have not attained the goal. This is why Paul said, "Not as though I had already attained, either were already perfect: but I follow after, if that I may apprehend that for which also I am apprehended of Christ Jesus" (Phil. 3:12, KJV). In other words, Paul was saying there was room for much improvement in his own life, even at the time he was writing to the Philippians.

Maturity in Christ

Notice Paul's expression: "Either were already perfect" (Phil. 3:12, KJV). Paul was not referring to a sinless perfection but to spiritual maturity. Even though he had founded the church in Philippi about 10 years earlier and had accomplished many significant acts in the meantime, Paul still felt he had a long way to go in the Christian life.

Paul was especially concerned that believers go on to maturity. Paul told the Corinthians, "And I, brethren, could not speak to you as to spiritual men, but as to men of flesh, as to babes in Christ. I gave you milk to drink, not solid food; for you were not yet able to receive it. Indeed, even now you are not yet able, for you are still fleshly. For since there is jealousy and strife among you, are you not fleshly, and are you not walking like mere men?" (I Cor. 3:1-3).

Personally, I believe Paul was also the writer to the Hebrews, who said, "Concerning him we have much to say, and it is hard to explain, since you have become dull of hearing. For though by this time you ought to be teachers, you have need again for some one to teach you the elementary principles of the oracles of God, and you have come to need milk and not solid food. For every one who partakes only of milk is not accustomed to the word of righteousness, for he is a babe. But solid food is for the mature, who because of practice have their senses trained to discern good and evil" (Heb. 5:11-14).

So as Paul wrote to the Philippians, he saw room for improvement in his own spiritual maturity, even though he had grown spiritually for many years. Notice the statements of Paul in his letters that indicate spiritual progress. In one of his earliest letters he wrote: "I am the least of the apostles, who am not fit to be called an apostle" (I Cor. 15:9). Later in life he wrote: "To me, the very least of all saints, this grace was given" (Eph. 3:8). And in one of his last letters before his death he wrote: "Christ Jesus came into the world to save sinners, among whom I am foremost of all" (I Tim. 1:15).

Perhaps you say, "That does not sound like spiritual growth—if anything, it sounds like he's going the other way!" But that's the secret. Most of us are too big for God, and that is why He cannot use us. But the more we humble ourselves in His presence and in the presence of the world, the more we will be used by Him. Only then will God really be able to accomplish His work in us and through us.

God's principle of working in our lives is stated in James 4:6,10: "But He gives a greater grace. Therefore it says, 'God is opposed to the proud, but gives grace to the humble.' ... Humble yourselves in the presence of the Lord, and He will exalt you."

The same principle is emphasized in I Peter 5:6: "Humble yourselves, therefore, under the mighty hand of God, that He may exalt you at the proper time." This principle is also an Old Testament concept. Isaiah 57:15 says, "For thus says the high and exalted One who lives forever, whose name is Holy, 'I dwell on a high and holy place, and also with the contrite and lowly of spirit in order to revive the spirit of the lowly and to revive the heart of the contrite.' " God lives in the heart of the humble, and He delights in using the humble person to accomplish His will.

As believers, our spiritual position in Christ is perfect, but our spiritual condition on this earth has room for much growth and improvement. Our salvation is complete in Christ, and it cannot be added to. There is "no condemnation for those who are in Christ Jesus" (Rom. 8:1).

The believer can also say, "What then shall we say to these things? If God is for us, who is against us? ... Who is the one who condemns? Christ Jesus is He who died, yes, rather who was raised, who is at the right hand of God, who also intercedes for us. Who shall separate us from the love of Christ? Shall tribulation, or distress, or persecution, or famine, or nakedness, or peril, or sword? ... For I am convinced that neither death, nor life, nor angels, nor principalities, nor things present, nor things to come, nor powers, nor height, nor depth, nor any other created thing, shall be able to separate us from the love of God, which is in Christ Jesus our Lord" (vv. 31,34,35,38,39).

So salvation, once entered into, is complete in Christ. Salvation itself cannot be added to or subtracted from. But spiritual growth in this life is quite another matter. Romans 8:32 indicates that God also gives us all we need for daily living: "He who did not spare His own Son, but delivered Him up for us all, how will He not also with Him freely give us all things?" Second Peter 1:3 emphasizes the same truth: "Seeing that His divine power has granted to us everything pertaining to life and godliness." So in our *position* we are complete, but in our *condition* we are being completed. The process goes on until we are conformed to the image of His Son (see Rom. 8:28,29).

Paul told the Philippians: "Not as though I had already attained, either were already perfect: but I follow after" (Phil. 3:12, KJV). The Greek word translated "I follow after" means "follow" in the sense of "pursue." Like a runner pursuing the goal, Paul wanted to honor Jesus Christ in everything he did so he would be more and more molded into the image of Jesus Christ.

But what was Paul pursuing? He said, "If that I may apprehend that for which also I am apprehended of Christ Jesus" (v. 12, KJV). He wanted to lay hold of—to grasp, to appropriate for himself—that which God had purposed when God called him.

In writing to the Galatians, Paul said, "But when He who had set me apart, even from my mother's womb, and called me through His grace, was pleased to reveal His Son in me, that I might preach Him among the Gentiles, I did not immediately consult with flesh and blood" (Gal. 1:15,16). From this passage we see that Paul was called to reveal Jesus Christ.

At the time of Paul's conversion, the Lord instructed Ananias to go to Paul. Ananias was hesitant to do so at first because he had heard of all the things Paul had done to Christians. But the Lord told Ananias, "Go, for he is a chosen instrument of Mine, to bear My name before the Gentiles and kings and the sons of Israel" (Acts 9:15). So Paul's calling—and ours—is to reveal Jesus Christ to others. At the time Paul was writing to the Philippians he did not believe he had accomplished all that God had intended for him when He had called him to salvation.

To become a Christian is not the end of God's purpose for us; it is only the beginning. Ephesians 2:10 emphasizes this further work: "For we are His workmanship, created in Christ Jesus for good works, which God prepared beforehand, that we should walk in them." The ultimate purpose is that we become like God's Son, Jesus Christ. Knowledge of this ultimate goal drives one on to attain, or to lay hold of, that goal.

Victory in Christ

Paul told the Philippians, "Brethren, I count not myself to have apprehended: but this one thing I do, forgetting those things which are behind, and reaching forth unto those things which are before, I press toward the mark for the prize of the high calling of God in Christ Jesus" (Phil. 3:13,14, KJV).

In these verses it is evident that Paul had a compulsion to go on to spiritual victories in Christ Jesus. Have you sometimes wondered, Where does this kind of a drive come from? Is it characteristic only of people like Paul, Moses and a few select others?

Let me answer that by asking another question: What drove God to provide salvation for us? He did not have to do so, but He did. The verse that most of us have known since childhood gives the answer: "For God so loved the world, that He gave His only begotten Son" (John 3:16).

The key is the kind of love God has for us. The Greek word translated "love" in John 3:16 is the verb form of *agape*. Although this love involves the emotions, it is more a love of the will than it is of the emotions. It is choosing to seek another person's highest good, and it is used frequently of God because this is the kind of nature He has. He is determined to exercise His love for us in spite of the fact that we do not deserve it.

This kind of love originates with God, not man. However, at the time of our salvation, God planted this kind of love in our hearts. This is the key to understanding the source of the kind of drive that Paul had. It is placed in the believer's life by the Holy Spirit. Romans 5:5 says, "The love of God has been poured out within our hearts through the Holy Spirit who was given to us."

Because of love like this Paul told the believers in Philippi, "Let this mind be in you, which was also in Christ Jesus" (Phil. 2:5, KJV). Because this kind of love had been placed in them by the Holy Spirit, Paul told the same believers, "Work out your own salvation with fear and trembling. For it is God which worketh in you both to will and to do" (Phil. 2:12,13, KJV).

So God's kind of love became our love when we were born again. It is this kind of love operating within us that makes us willing, makes us want, to do God's will and also energizes us to do it. So it is not our love that drives us on, it is His love. As Paul said in II Corinthians 5:14, "The love of Christ controls us." That is, Christ's love urges, or impels, us on.

If we live other than the way Paul did—if we do not want to apprehend that for which we have been apprehended—we nullify the love of God which is in our hearts. What causes us to be so unconcerned that we nullify God's love? It is our allowing the self-life to have the upper hand in our lives.

Just as one chemical can be used to neutralize another chemical, so there are things in our lives that neutralize the love of God in our hearts. Perhaps one of the most prevalent attitudes today that neutralizes God's love is that of materialism. Materialistic desires often go extremely opposite to the desires of God as expressed by His love. God forbids us to be controlled by a materialistic attitude; He wants us to be controlled by His love. Instead of letting a materialistic philosophy possess our lives, we should let the mind of Christ possess us. The result of having His kind of mind will be having His kind of love.

We quench the Holy Spirit by allowing the self-life with its materialistic attitude to nullify the love of God which is in our hearts. If we have trusted Christ as Saviour, His love is embedded there by the Holy Spirit, waiting to have a chance to operate in our lives.

The Apostle Paul was a man of purpose. He said, "This one thing I do" (Phil. 3:13, KJV). Paul knew the purpose for which God had apprehended him, and he knew that he was a citizen of heaven (see v. 20). Paul was determined, therefore, to fulfill everything God had in mind for him. He had specifically been called to reveal Christ (see Gal. 1:16), and he considered himself—and all believers—to be an ambassador for Jesus Christ. "We are ambassadors for Christ, as though God were entreating through us; we beg you on behalf of Christ, be reconciled to God" (II Cor. 5:20).

Paul wanted to be an effective, functioning member of the Body of Christ. Christ has two bodies. He has a physical body, which He acquired when He was born into this world that He might live a perfect life and die for the sins of the world. His physical body is now glorified, and He is sitting at the right hand of the Father. Christ also has a mystical Body—believers everywhere are referred to as being a part of His Body. This Body is also known as "the Church." Ephesians 1:22,23 says that Jesus Christ is "head over all things to the church, which is his body." Each believer is a member of Christ's Body. Paul said, "For even as the body is one and yet has many members, and all the members of the body, though they are many, are one body, so also is Christ. For by one Spirit we were all baptized into one body" (I Cor. 12:12,13).

Each individual believer is also a temple of God because God resides in the believer. Believers are told: "Do you not know that your body is a temple of the Holy Spirit who is in you, whom you have from God, and that you are not your own? For you have been bought with a price: therefore glorify God in your body" (6:19,20).

No wonder Paul was motivated to grasp and accomplish everything for which God had called him.

In Philippians 3:13 the words "I do" are in italics in the King James Version, indicating they were added by the translators in order to give a fuller sense. Paul's emphasis, however, was on the words "one thing." He was intent on accomplishing one thing, and that one motivating goal was wrapped up in the Person of Christ—first, last and always. Does God expect the same of us? Inasmuch as God gave His Son because He loved us, can we do less than allow His love to operate in our lives? God is not looking for great ability or great knowledge. These qualities are not bad in themselves, but the one element God is looking for is the person who is totally consumed with Him.

Threefold Action

Paul's concentration on the Person of Christ activated a threefold action.

Forgetting the Past

First, there was a past aspect: "Forgetting those things which are behind" (Phil. 3:13, KJV). Before we can reach any great height in life, we have to deal with the past. It was not that Paul was trying not to remember; rather, he was deliberately forgetting the past. He was not simply attempting to glibly cross out the past by wishful thinking and go on as if nothing had happened, but he dealt with the past.

We can do nothing about the past except make necessary confession. And when confession is made, the Bible promises: "If we confess our sins, He is faithful and righteous to forgive us our sins and to cleanse us from all unrighteousness" (I John 1:9). By confession, sin is placed under the cleansing blood of the Lord Jesus Christ, and when it is under the blood, it does not condemn any longer. Unless the past is dealt with, one is not prepared to live in the present nor to go on into the future. Unless the past is dealt with, it becomes a haunting memory that saps the strength of the believer so he is unable to honor Christ in his daily life.

What God does with sin when it is confessed is explained in various passages. Isaiah 44:22 says, "I have wiped out your transgressions like a thick cloud, and your sins like a heavy mist. Return to Me, for I have redeemed you." Hebrews 8:12 says, "For I will be merciful to their iniquities, and I will remember their sins no more."

Someone has said, "The present must forget the past by correction, or else the past will become a moral and spiritual liability for the future."

Consider some items that need to be forgotten: failures—they keep our faith from advancing; successes—they create pride (see Prov. 16:18); losses—they drag us down so we cannot serve the Lord the way we should; grievances—they produce false attitudes (see I Cor. 13:6); sorrows—God can heal all heartaches; discouragements—we need to remember Christ, not disappointments, thwarted hopes and plans.

We must remember that sin is wrong and cannot be forgotten merely by dismissing it; it must be dealt with according to I John 1:9. And when sin has been dealt with by confessing it, we should not make God a liar by saying, "I don't think God has forgiven me." God has promised that if we confess, He forgives, and we need to take Him at His word.

Reaching Forth in the Present

Having emphasized that he was doing one thing and having mentioned the aspect of the past ("forgetting those things which are behind"), Paul then mentioned the aspect of the present: "And reaching forth unto those things which are before" (Phil. 3:13, KJV).

All of this passage is interrelated and, in a sense, what Paul was reaching forward to grasp was what he had already stated in verse 10: "That I may know him, and the power of his resurrection, and the fellowship of his sufferings, being made conformable unto his death" (KJV). Paul wanted to know Christ as the secret of his daily walk. The possibilities in Christ are unlimited, so we need to know Him for who He is and for what He is.

In Old Testament times, God had to especially emphasize His people's need to know Him because they did not have as much revealed information about God as we do. God told Moses: "I am the Lord; and I appeared to Abraham, Isaac, and Jacob, as God Almighty, but by My name, Lord, I did not make Myself known to them" (Ex. 6:2,3). At the burning bush, God revealed Himself to Moses as "I Am Who I Am" (3:14). Because God is eternal, He will be to us at any moment all that we need to the limit of all that He is. He is our God, our life, our power—our everything.

Pressing Toward the Future

The Apostle Paul's "one thing"(Phil 3:13, KJV) had not only past and present aspects but also a future one: "I press toward the mark for the prize of the high calling of God in Christ Jesus" (v. 14, KJV).

The intensity with which Paul was moving toward his goal is seen in the word he used for "press." The word is the same one that is translated "follow after" in verse 12, and it refers to an intense pursuit.

Paul was pursuing "the mark" (v. 14, KJV). Along with everything else it might include, the most important was Christlikeness. Paul's burning desire was to be molded into the image of Jesus Christ, and he realized that was God's ultimate purpose (see Rom. 8:28,29).

It is good to underscore again that salvation is not our ultimate goal. It is only the foundation. It is a shame that some believers in this life never get beyond the foundation of their salvation. We need to establish that the foundation is Christ (see I Cor. 3:11), and when we are in right relationship to Christ, we have salvation. But that is only the beginning; we need to go on "toward the mark for the prize of the high calling of God in Christ Jesus" (Phil. 3:14, KJV).

It is apparent that Paul's desire was not just to be saved from condemnation; he also wanted to go on to spiritual maturity and to finish his course with joy (see Acts 20:24). The manner in which Paul finished his course is seen from the last letter we have from his pen, II Timothy. Paul told Timothy, "For I am already being poured out as a drink offering, and the time of my departure has come. I have fought the good fight, I have finished the course, I have kept the faith; in the future there is laid up for me the crown of righteousness, which the Lord, the righteous Judge, will award to me on that day; and not only to me, but also to all who have loved His appearing" (4:6-8).

Even as Paul started his letter to the Philippians, he emphasized that Christ was everything to him (see Phil. 1:21). He was writing about a future goal, however, when he said, "I press toward the mark for the prize of the high calling of God in Christ Jesus" (3:14, KJV).

The prize Paul was striving for was not heaven. Heaven is not won by striving but by grace; it is the gift of God. Paul's goal was to be like Christ. For Christ, after humiliation came triumph, glory, honor and exaltation. Even for himself, Paul believed that after suffering would come exaltation.

In Paul's last letter, he wrote: "If we endure, we shall also reign with Him" (II Tim. 2:12). The Book of the Revelation also has many promises to the one who overcomes, such as, "To him who overcomes, I will grant to eat of the tree of life,

which is in the Paradise of God" (2:7). (See also 2:26,27;
3:5,12,21.)

As the New Testament tells of the need to look to the
future, it uses Moses as an example: "By faith Moses, when
he had grown up, refused to be called the son of Pharaoh's
daughter; choosing rather to endure ill-treatment with the
people of God, than to enjoy the passing pleasures of sin;
considering the reproach of Christ greater riches than the
treasures of Egypt; for he was looking to the reward" (Heb.
11:24-26).

As Paul looked ahead toward his goal, he told Timothy,
"The Lord will deliver me from every evil deed, and will
bring me safely to His heavenly kingdom" (II Tim. 4:18).
Paul had assurance that he would eventually be in the very
presence of Christ, and that is why he desired so much to be
conformed to the image of Christ even while living on this
earth. Paul had the confidence, even as expressed by John:
"We know that, when He appears, we shall be like Him,
because we shall see Him just as He is. And every one who
has this hope fixed on Him purifies himself, just as He is
pure" (I John 3:2,3).

Christ is the author and perfecter of our faith (see Heb.
12:2), and Paul's goal was to be like Jesus Christ. Paul
wanted to know Him well so that he could reign with Christ
later. Paul wanted to put all of his sins under the blood of
Christ in this life so as to experience more reward and blessing in the future.

Exhortation to Like-mindedness

Paul told the Philippians, "Let us therefore, as many as be
perfect, be thus minded: and if in any thing ye be otherwise
minded, God shall reveal even this unto you. Nevertheless,
whereto we have already attained, let us walk by the same
rule, let us mind the same thing" (Phil. 3:15,16, KJV).

On the surface these verses seem to present a contradic-
tion. In verse 12 Paul indicated he was not "perfect," but in
verse 15 he addressed remarks to "as many as be perfect"
(KJV).

There are two different aspects of being perfect. There is
the judicial aspect in which a person is declared perfect at the

time of salvation when the righteousness of Christ is placed on his account. This is the perfection Paul spoke of in verse 15. But there is also an experiential aspect, which is a maturing in the Christian life, and this is what Paul referred to in verse 12. So even though a person is not perfect in action in this life, he is perfect in his standing in Jesus Christ, having trusted Christ as Saviour.

Paul wanted the Philippians to be like-minded concerning the things he had said in verses 10-14. He wanted them to have the same convictions that he had. And he expressed to them that if their attitude of mind was different, God could change it. As believers, we are endowed with the mind of Christ, so we are to let His way of thinking change our minds so we will think as He wants us to. Thus, God can and will reveal to us where our minds fall short of having the same attitude that Christ had.

Paul was concerned that the Philippians not slip back from that which they had already attained: "Nevertheless, whereto we have already attained, let us walk by the same rule, let us mind the same thing" (v. 16, KJV). Paul assured the Philippians that they would succeed in the race as they maintained a right walk (see 2:12).

Paul was urging the Philippians to hold fast, even as the Book of the Revelation instructs: "Nevertheless what you have, hold fast until I come" (2:25). "I am coming quickly; hold fast what you have, in order that no one take your crown" (3:11). But along with these exhortations there is also a warning: "Remember therefore what you have received and heard; and keep it, and repent. If therefore you will not wake up, I will come like a thief, and you will not know at what hour I will come upon you" (v. 3).

Paul's concern for the Philippians is seen clearly in the way the New International Version renders Philippians 3:16: "Only let us live up to what we have already attained."

Paul urged the Philippians to follow him: "Brethren, be followers together of me, and mark them which walk so as ye have us for an ensample" (v. 17, KJV). Paul was not evidencing a spirit of pride as he enjoined the Philippians to imitate his example; he had already expressed that he was following Christ. Paul made no claim to be perfect or to have already arrived at his goal; in fact, he declared the opposite (see v. 12).

Paul wanted the Philippians to be totally committed to Christ even as he was committed to Him. He was not necessarily encouraging the Philippians to mimic his specific actions—although they were honorable ones—but he wanted them to follow his example of totally following Christ. It is the same thought he wrote to the Corinthians: "Be imitators of me, just as I also am of Christ" (I Cor. 11:1).

Although Paul was an example to be followed, there were also some examples to be shunned. Paul told the Philippians, "For many walk, of whom I have told you often, and now tell you even weeping, that they are the enemies of the cross of Christ: whose end is destruction, whose God is their belly, and whose glory is in their shame, who mind earthly things" (Phil. 3:18,19, KJV).

The people Paul referred to are those who deny God's power and follow man-made rules. Paul told the Colossians, "See to it that no one takes you captive through philosophy and empty deception, according to the tradition of men, according to the elementary principles of the world, rather than according to Christ" (Col. 2:8). There are those who allow Christian liberty to degenerate into license to sin. Paul warned, "For you were called to freedom, brethren; only do not turn your freedom into an opportunity for the flesh, but through love serve one another" (Gal. 5:13).

The kind of people Paul was warning the Philippians about did not understand God's grace and thus thought lightly of continuing in sin. In this regard, Paul told the Romans, "What shall we say then? Are we to continue in sin that grace might increase? May it never be! How shall we who died to sin still live in it?" (Rom. 6:1,2). Paul also asked, "What then? Shall we sin because we are not under law but under grace? May it never be!" (v. 15).

Those whom Paul warned the Philippians against were also engrossed in self-indulgence. There are examples in Scripture of the judgment of God that falls on those engulfed in self-indulgence. One such example is that of Eli's sons, Hophni and Phinehas, who were the unspiritual sons of a godly father. Read I Samuel 2:12-36 and be impressed with the fact that the judgment of God finally falls on those who are engrossed in self-indulgence.

Object of the Believer's Expectation

The last two verses of Philippians 3 present Christ as the object of the believer's expectation. "For our conversation is in heaven; from whence also we look for the Saviour, the Lord Jesus Christ: who shall change our vile body, that it may be fashioned like unto his glorious body, according to the working whereby he is able even to subdue all things unto himself" (vv. 20,21, KJV).

These verses focus attention on the day when the believer will stand before Christ. At the beginning of Paul's letter to the Philippians he said, "Being confident of this very thing, that he which hath begun a good work in you will perform it until the day of Jesus Christ" (1:6, KJV). Paul was talking about that day in 3:20,21. The picture is that of a beautiful life ahead.

The Christian life begins with Christ as its author, with a constant looking to Christ as its life (1:21) and its mind (2:5) and its constant goal (3:10). It concludes with Christ as the finisher, as Hebrews 12:2 says: "Looking unto Jesus the author and finisher of our faith" (KJV).

In concluding our study of Philippians 3 we note a summarizing of the past, present and future of the Christian walk. Sometimes this walk is referred to as a "race" because there are so many similarities between a race and the Christian life. For instance, both are directed toward a goal.

Heavenly Citizenship

Paul said, "For our conversation is in heaven" (Phil. 3:20, KJV). The word "conversation" means "citizenship." Although this was a present possession of the Philippians, they had entered into it in the past by their decision to trust Christ as Saviour. Therefore, we think of it as a past aspect that has been entered into by the believer.

When Jesus was on earth, He said, "In My Father's house are many dwelling places; if it were not so, I would have told you; for I go to prepare a place for you" (John 14:2). Inasmuch as heaven is the home for the believer, he is considered a pilgrim and a stranger here on earth. Peter exhorted believers, "Beloved, I urge you as aliens and strangers to abstain from fleshly lusts, which wage war against the soul" (I Pet. 2:11). The great faith chapter, Hebrews 11, refers to the Old Testament patriarchs as being strangers on earth: "All these died in faith, without receiving the promises, but having seen them and having welcomed them from a distance, and having confessed that they were strangers and exiles on the earth" (v. 13).

All of us who have believed in Christ, like the patriarchs, are "looking for the city which has foundations, whose architect and builder is God" (v. 10). Believers of old were "seeking a country of their own" (v. 14), and we, too, are seeking a heavenly country. Even though we reside on earth, our legal residence is in heaven.

Therefore, our minds should be on that which originates in heaven rather than on that which originates on earth. Paul told of those whose minds were on earthly things. He referred to them as "enemies of the cross of Christ, whose end is destruction, whose god is their appetite, and whose glory is in their shame, who set their minds on earthly things" (Phil. 3:18,19). In contrast to this kind of people, the believer is to follow the injunctions of Colossians 3:1-3: "If then you have been raised up with Christ, keep seeking the things above, where Christ is, seated at the right hand of God. Set your mind on the things above, not on the things that are on earth. For you have died and your life is hidden with Christ in God."

Jesus Himself prayed, "Thy will be done, on earth as it is in heaven" (Matt. 6:10). Jesus was concerned about God's will being carried out not just in the end times but also now in the believer. So whereas the pattern of our life is heavenly, the practice is here on earth. We are enrolled and registered in heaven, and we possess all the privileges of heaven. But although our names are written in the books of heaven, we are pilgrims and strangers here on earth. Even as Abraham, Isaac and Jacob demonstrated that they were strangers by living in tents (see Heb. 11:9), there should be things about us to indicate to others that our real citizenship is in heaven.

Realizing what the future holds should cause us to live

pure lives. This is evident from II Peter 3:10-14: "But the day of the Lord will come like a thief, in which the heavens will pass away with a roar and the elements will be destroyed with intense heat, and the earth and its works will be burned up. Since all these things are to be destroyed in this way, what sort of people ought you to be in holy conduct and godliness, looking for and hastening the coming of the day of God, on account of which the heavens will be destroyed by burning, and the elements will melt with intense heat! But according to His promise we are looking for new heavens and a new earth, in which righteousness dwells. Therefore, beloved, since you look for these things, be diligent to be found by Him in peace, spotless and blameless."

Importance of Citizenship

As Paul wrote to the Philippians and emphasized that the believer's citizenship is in heaven (Phil. 3:20), there would surely have been some among his readers who would have remembered the issue made concerning his citizenship when he first came to Philippi. He and Silas had been thrown into prison by the city officials. The day after an earthquake opened the prison doors, the officials sent word to release Paul and Silas. However, Paul said, "They have beaten us in public without trial, men who are Romans, and have thrown us into prison; and now are they sending us away secretly? No indeed! But let them come themselves and bring us out" (Acts 16:37).

When the city officials learned that Paul and Silas were Roman citizens, they became very concerned and appealed to them to please leave the city. Before they left, Paul and Silas went to the house of Lydia and encouraged the Christians there. Paul's Roman citizenship protected him against such abuse.

Another incident in Paul's life reveals the importance of Roman citizenship. "The commander ordered him to be brought into the barracks, stating that he should be examined by scourging so that he might find out the reason why they were shouting against him that way. And when they stretched him out with thongs, Paul said to the centurion who was standing by, 'Is it lawful for you to scourge a man who is a Roman and uncondemned?' And when the centurion heard this, he went to the commander and told him, saying, 'What are you about to do? For this man is a Roman.' And the commander came and said to him, 'Tell me, are you a Roman?' And he said, 'Yes.' And the commander answered, 'I acquired this citizenship with a large sum of money.' And Paul said, 'But I was actually born a citizen' " (22:24-28).

The Philippians would have been well aware of the importance of citizenship, so Paul's statement that the citizenship of believers is in heaven (Phil. 3:20) would have been especially significant to them. Although we are citizens of heaven, we should not expect good treatment on this earth. Jesus said, "These things I have spoken to you, that in Me you may have peace. In the world you have tribulation, but take courage; I have overcome the world" (John 16:33). Even though the world abuses the believer, the Christian is not to be lawless or insubordinate to earthly governments (see Rom. 13:1-7).

There is a parallel between an ambassador of a country as he lives in a foreign country and the believer who is a citizen of heaven living on earth. A United States ambassador receives the protection of the American flag while he is on foreign soil. This does not mean he will be free from difficulty, but it does mean he has the authority and protection of his own country behind him in case anything happens. So, too, the believer experiences difficulties on earth, but he has the authority of heaven behind him, and eventually he will be rewarded, and those who persecuted him will be judged.

It is important that we whose citizenship is in heaven do not mimic the standards of this world which we are passing through. It is regrettable that so many Christians reflect the value systems of the world in their possessions, entertainment and music. We must be careful to always realize that this is not our real home; we are citizens of heaven. Thus, we should make sure that our values have the right priorities. Jesus said, "Do not lay up for yourselves treasures upon earth, where moth and rust destroy, and where thieves break in and steal. But lay up for yourselves treasures in heaven, where neither moth nor rust destroys, and where thieves do not break in or steal; for where your treasure is, there will your heart be also" (Matt. 6:19-21).

Because so many people are dropping out of their thinking the truths of eternity, immorality and heaven, we are fast becoming a generation of earth-bound pagans. As we have grown older, my wife and I often say, "I just don't feel at home down here on this earth anymore." The wickedness of the present generation seems to far exceed the wickedness of Sodom and Gomorrah, upon which God rained fire and brimstone.

The Believer's Present Attitude

Having mentioned that our citizenship is in heaven, Paul then mentioned the present aspect of believers: "From whence also we look for the Saviour, the Lord Jesus Christ" (Phil. 3:20, KJV). This is to be our present attitude in view of Christ's return from heaven.

Jesus said, "In My Father's house are many dwelling places; if it were not so, I would have told you; for I go to prepare a place for you. And if I go and prepare a place for you, I will come again, and receive you to Myself; that where I am, there you may be also" (John 14:2,3). As Jesus was ascending into heaven, angelic beings told the disciples, "Men of Galilee, why do you stand looking into the sky? This Jesus, who has been taken up from you into heaven, will come in just the same way as you have watched Him go into heaven" (Acts 1:11).

As we watch and wait for the Saviour to return, we should not fasten our eyes on the clouds with an attitude of idleness but with much activity and a constant expectancy that He may return at any moment. Just as the nobleman told his servants: "Occupy till I come" (Luke 19:13, KJV), so we need to faithfully be involved with the business of the Lord until he returns. Believers are to be like faithful stewards who heed the command: "Be dressed in readiness, and keep your lamps alight. And be like men who are waiting for their master when he returns from the wedding feast, so that they may immediately open the door to him when he comes and knocks" (Luke 12:35,36).

As to the return of the Lord, we should be waiting, watching and doing. Jesus said, "Blessed are those servants, whom the lord when he cometh shall find watching: verily I say unto you, that he shall gird himself, and make them to sit down to meat, and will come forth and serve them" (v. 37, KJV).

Jesus also said, "Who then is the faithful and sensible steward, whom his master will put in charge of his servants, to give them their rations at the proper time? Blessed is that slave whom his master finds so doing when he comes" (vv. 42,43).

It is a sure hope that Christ will return for the believer. Hebrews 9:28 says, "So Christ also, having been offered once to bear the sins of many, shall appear a second time, not to bear sin, to those who eagerly await Him, for salvation."

Throughout the Scriptures, the Lord's return is presented as an incentive to better living (see I John 3:2,3). Those who are looking for Him will experience joy when they meet Him face to face. But those who are not looking for Him will discover it to be an awesome time as they stand before Him to give account (see II Cor. 5:10,11). If we have been unfaithful in this life, we will not look forward to Christ's coming. If we have honored Him to the depths of our ability, it will be a joyous time.

As we wait for the Lord, are we occupied with His business while we anticipate His coming? Whether we are living when He returns and are taken immediately to meet Him in the air or whether we die in the meantime and are resurrected at His coming, our attitude now should be one of spiritual preparedness. Throughout the ages, believers have looked for Christ, and it has stimulated their behavior.

Effects of Christ's Coming

Paul told the believers in Philippi what Jesus would do when He returned: "Who shall change our vile body, that it may be fashioned like unto his glorious body, according to the working whereby he is able even to subdue all things unto himself" (Phil. 3:21, KJV). In this verse we see the twofold effect of Christ's coming—the changing of our bodies and the subduing of all things.

There is a prospective glory for those who are born again.

It is important to observe from the Scriptures that salvation actually has three aspects. There is the initial aspect of belief. Paul and Silas told the Philippian jailer, "Believe in the Lord Jesus, and you shall be saved, you and your household" (Acts 16:31). There is also the progressive aspect of salvation, as revealed in Philippians 2:12: "Work out your own salvation with fear and trembling" (KJV). Then there is the final aspect of salvation, which is the climax of it all—the finished product. This happens at the redemption of the body and is spoken of in Philippians 3:21: "Who shall change our vile body, that it may be fashioned like unto his glorious body" (KJV). This final step in salvation is also spoken of in Romans 8:23: "And not only this, but also we ourselves, having the first fruits of the Spirit, even we ourselves groan within ourselves, waiting eagerly for our adoption as sons, the redemption of our body."

The final aspect of salvation—the redemption of the body—is also referred to in I Corinthians 15:50-53: "Now I say this, brethren, that flesh and blood cannot inherit the kingdom of God; nor does the perishable inherit the imperishable. Behold, I tell you a mystery; we shall not all sleep, but we shall all be changed, in a moment, in the twinkling of an eye, at the last trumpet; for the trumpet will sound, and the dead will be raised imperishable, and we shall be changed. For this perishable must put on the imperishable, and this mortal must put on immortality."

The climax of the Christian experience is the complement of Christ's experience referred to in Philippians 2:5-11. There was first humiliation, then exaltation. In His humiliation, He came to share our likeness on earth. In the exaltation, He eagerly awaits our sharing His likeness in glory. Thus, Christ prayed, "Father, I desire that they also, whom Thou hast given Me, be with Me where I am, in order that they may behold My glory, which Thou hast given Me; for Thou didst love Me before the foundation of the world" (John 17:24).

That Jesus is eagerly awaiting our sharing His likeness in glory is also seen from John 14:3: "And if I go and prepare a place for you, I will come again, and receive you to Myself; that where I am, there you may be also." The body of our humiliation—"our vile body" (Phil. 3:21, KJV)—will be changed at the return of Christ. Ours are bodies of limitation now, but they shall be changed and conformed to the heavenly environment when Christ returns. Our bodies will be "fashioned like unto his glorious body" (v. 21, KJV). This is also emphasized in I Corinthians 15:54: "But when this perishable will have put on the imperishable, and this mortal will have put on immortality, then will come about the saying that is written, 'Death is swallowed up in victory.' "

The change, or glory, of the body of Christ was seen on the Mount of Transfiguration. Jesus brought Peter, James and John to a mountain, "and He was transfigured before them; and His face shone like the sun, and His garments became as white as light" (Matt. 17:2). The change of the body is also seen in Christ's resurrected body. After His resurrection, Christ was on earth for 40 days, and we learn much about His body during that time. He could pass through closed doors, His body had substance, He had bones, He ate, He talked. For more details, read Luke 24:36-43 and John 20:19,20. Gravity had no effect on His body; He was above the natural laws of the universe.

Someday we will have a body "fashioned like unto his glorious body, according to the working whereby he is able even to subdue all things unto himself" (Phil. 3:21, KJV). The word "subdue" means "set in array"; that is, to put all things in place.

When Christ comes to earth to rule the world, swords and spears will be beat into plowshares and pruning hooks (see Mic. 4:3). War will be replaced with His peaceful rule. He will set things in proper array and will rule with total authority. Righteousness will reign, and ungodliness will be brought into subjection. The world has never before known a government of absolute justice, equity and righteousness, as well as unqualified security.

Thinking about the time when the Lord will return to accomplish all of this, the Apostle John wrote: "And he said to me, 'Do not seal up the words of the prophecy of this book, for the time is near. Let the one who does wrong, still do wrong; and let the one who is filthy, still be filthy; and let the one who is righteous, still practice righteousness; and let the one who is holy, still keep himself holy. Behold, I am coming quickly, and My reward is with Me, to render to every man according to what he has done. I am the Alpha and the

Omega, the first and the last, the beginning and the end.' ...
And the Spirit and the bride say, 'Come.' And let the one who
hears say, 'Come.' And let the one who is thirsty come; let the
one who wishes take the water of life without cost" (Rev.
22:10-13,17).

What a glorious time that will be! How wonderful it is to be
able to say with the Apostle John: "Even so, come, Lord
Jesus" (v. 20, KJV).

Chapter 7

Christ Our Strength

Having seen that Christ is our life (Phil. 1), our mind (ch. 2) and our goal (ch. 3), we now see that Christ is our strength (ch. 4). The key verse of this chapter is verse 13: "I can do all things through Christ which strengtheneth me" (KJV).

There are five commands in the first eight verses of Philippians 4 (KJV): "Stand fast in the Lord" (v. 1); "Rejoice in the Lord alway" (v. 4); "Let your moderation be known unto all men" (v. 5); "Be careful for nothing" (v. 6); "Think on these things" (v. 8).

The fourth chapter begins with the words "Therefore, my brethren, dearly beloved and longed for, my joy and crown, so stand fast in the Lord, my dearly beloved" (v. 1, KJV). The word "therefore" indicates that Paul was referring to all he had said previously, which is summarized by the key verses indicating that Christ is our life (1:21), mind (2:5) and goal (3:10). As indicated, we learn in this chapter that Christ is also our strength (4:13).

An emphatic statement by Paul that has a sobering effect on all that is said in Philippians is "the Lord is at hand" (v. 5, KJV). This statement may refer to the Second Coming of Christ, which may occur at any time. The first aspect of the Second Coming will be the believers' being caught up to meet the Lord in the air (see I Thess. 4:13-18). At that time the Judgment Seat of Christ, where rewards are distributed to believers, will occur (see II Cor. 5:9-11). This will mean a release from present suffering and trials (see I Pet. 1:5-7).

It is also possible that the phrase "the Lord is at hand" may refer to His constant presence with the believer. Although either interpretation is acceptable, I prefer the latter one because of the emphasis of the Book of Philippians.

While Jesus was yet on earth, He said, "And I will ask the Father, and He will give you another Helper, that He may be with you forever; that is the Spirit of truth, whom the world cannot receive, because it does not behold Him or know Him, but you know Him because He abides with you, and will be in you. I will not leave you as orphans; I will come to you" (John 14:16-18).

That the Lord is with us at all times is also seen from the Great Commission, in which He commanded, "Go therefore and make disciples of all the nations, baptizing them in the name of the Father and the Son and the Holy Spirit, teaching them to observe all that I commanded you; and lo, I am with you always, even to the end of the age" (Matt. 28:19,20).

Paul had also learned by experience that the Lord was always present with him. During his trial in Jerusalem, which eventually led to his imprisonment in Rome, the Bible states, "But on the night immediately following, the Lord stood at his side and said, 'Take courage; for as you have solemnly witnessed to My cause at Jerusalem, so you must witness at Rome also' " (Acts 23:11). And while on his way to Rome, Paul was used of the Lord to encourage the people on board the ship. One of the remarks he made to them was "For this very night an angel of the God to whom I belong and whom I serve stood before me, saying, 'Do not be afraid, Paul; you must stand before Caesar; and behold, God has granted you all those who are sailing with you' " (27:23,24).

So Paul was well aware that "the Lord is at hand" (Phil. 4:5) in the sense that the Lord is always with the believer. The Lord is always available and is a constant presence to strengthen us. This parallels the key verse of Chapter 4: "I can do all things through Christ which strengtheneth me" (v. 13, KJV).

Remember, Paul wrote these words from a Roman imprisonment, but his confinement took on new characteristics as Paul realized "the Lord is at hand."

"Stand Fast"

In all of this we see the sufficiency of Christ for our steadfastness. He is at hand to provide all we need. The secret of
this security is stated in Philippians 4:1: "Stand fast in the
Lord" (KJV). Connecting the thoughts of verses 1 and 5
reveals how we find the Lord to be sufficient in all things.

Notice that verse 1 says we are to "stand fast." It does not
say we are to "stand still." When the Old Testament Israelites were being delivered from Egypt, they were fleeing from
the land with the Egyptians pursuing them, the mountains
on one side, the desert on the other and the Red Sea in front of
them. Through Moses, God instructed Israel, "Fear ye not,
stand still, and see the salvation of the Lord, which he will
shew to you to day: for the Egyptians whom ye have seen to
day, ye shall see them again no more for ever. The Lord shall
fight for you, and ye shall hold your peace" (Ex. 14:13,14,
KJV).

In a sense, the Israelites were spiritual babes at that time,
whereas the Philippian believers were growing, mature
Christians. The responsibility of the Philippians, therefore,
was to "stand fast," or to "stand firm," in the Lord. They
were to have an unwavering, unchanging faith and to be
determined in their purpose. They were not to be like new
Christians. Similarly, Paul told the Ephesian believers, "As
a result, we are no longer to be children, tossed here and there
by waves, and carried about by every wind of doctrine, by the
trickery of men, by craftiness in deceitful scheming" (Eph.
4:14). Instead, Paul said, "But speaking the truth in love, we
are to grow up in all aspects into Him, who is the head, even
Christ" (v. 15).

Paul also addressed mature Christians as he wrote to the
believers in Colossae. He instructed them, "As you therefore
have received Christ Jesus the Lord, so walk in Him, having
been firmly rooted and now being built up in Him and established in your faith, just as you were instructed, and overflowing with gratitude. . . . And in Him you have been made
complete, and He is the head over all rule and authority"
(Col. 2:6,7,10).

By standing firm in Christ, we go on to even greater spiritual maturity. So the secret of steadfastness is to "stand fast

in the Lord" (Phil. 4:1, KJV). This can be done only by daily fellowship, meditation, prayer, faith and obedience. It is not done by some magic, or special, formula; it is a moment-by-moment growth in Christ's life through the Word. The only way we can grow in the knowledge of Christ is to grow in our knowledge of the Word.

A ministry of the Word of God to believers has taken various forms down through the centuries. But regardless of the form, each person who goes to the Word with an open heart benefits greatly. On one occasion when David was being confronted by his own men because all of their families had been captured by the enemy, the Bible states, "Moreover David was greatly distressed because the people spoke of stoning him, for all the people were embittered, each one because of his sons and his daughters. But David strengthened himself in the Lord his God" (I Sam. 30:6). This was the benefit of the Word of God to David in his time of crisis.

Notice what personal worship meant to the psalmist: "I waited patiently for the Lord; and He inclined to me, and heard my cry. He brought me up out of the pit of destruction, out of the miry clay; and He set my feet upon a rock making my footsteps firm. And He put a new song in my mouth, a song of praise to our God" (Ps. 40:1-3).

The longest psalm, Psalm 119, also reveals the preciousness of the Word of God to the psalmist: "O how I love Thy law! It is my meditation all the day. Thy commandments make me wiser than my enemies, for they are ever mine. I have more insight than all my teachers, for Thy testimonies are my meditation. I understand more than the aged, because I have observed Thy precepts. I have restrained my feet from every evil way, that I may keep Thy word. I have not turned aside from Thine ordinances, for Thou Thyself hast taught me. How sweet are Thy words to my taste! Yes, sweeter than honey to my mouth! From Thy precepts I get understanding; therefore I hate every false way" (vv. 97-104).

The characteristics of the person who is feeding upon God's Word are seen in Psalm 1:2,3: "But his delight is in the law of the Lord, and in His law he meditates day and night.

And he will be like a tree firmly planted by streams of water."

Paul's exhortation to the Philippians to "stand fast in the Lord" (Phil. 4:1, KJV) is found frequently in the Scriptures. Ephesians 6:13,14 says, "Therefore, take up the full armor of God, that you may be able to resist in the evil day, and having done everything, to stand firm. Stand firm therefore, having girded your loins with truth, and having put on the breastplate of righteousness." First Corinthians 16:13 says, "Be on the alert, stand firm in the faith, act like men, be strong."

Galatians 5:1 says, "It was for freedom that Christ set us free; therefore keep standing firm and do not be subject again to a yoke of slavery." First Peter 5:8,9 says, "Be of sober spirit, be on the alert. Your adversary, the devil, prowls about like a roaring lion, seeking someone to devour. But resist him, firm in your faith, knowing that the same experiences of suffering are being accomplished by your brethren who are in the world."

"Be of the Same Mind"

Having urged all of the believers in Philippi to stand fast, Paul then addressed two specific individuals: "I beseech Euodias, and beseech Syntyche, that they be of the same mind in the Lord" (Phil. 4:2, KJV). These two women had developed some differences "in the Lord," but Paul does not specifically state the problems. Instead of their having differences "in the Lord," Paul wanted them to be "of the same mind in the Lord." Two people who differ cannot both have the mind of Christ. There are differences of function within the Body of Christ, as indicated by I Corinthians 12, but we are not to have a different manner of thinking. To be united in Christ's mind will not bring divisions but harmony. The Holy Spirit unites; He does not divide.

Paul's expression "in the Lord" (Phil. 4:2, KJV) means that Christ had one mind, which both of these women needed to seek and to be possessed by.

The Bible teaches that believers are individual members of one Body (see I Cor. 12). As long as those members are under the control of Christ, they will function harmoniously. So the remedy of any disunity is to be of the same mind as the Lord. This does not mean that believers will necessarily agree on every detail, but it means they will have a Christlike attitude and their differences will not divide. This was what Paul was beseeching Euodias and Syntyche to be like as he said, "I plead with Euodia and I plead with Syntyche to agree with each other in the Lord" (Phil. 4:2, NIV).

Paul believed the need for these women to come to common terms was so urgent that he even sought outside help: "And I intreat thee also, true yokefellow, help those women which laboured with me in the gospel, with Clement also, and with other my fellowlabourers, whose names are in the book of life" (v. 3, KJV).

These women were not new Christians; they had labored with Paul in the gospel. They had been co-workers with the veteran apostle, yet something or someone had divided them so they were no longer able to work together. Their differences needed to be healed not only for their own sakes but also for the sake of the Christian witness in Philippi. Paul was not questioning the salvation of these two women who had labored with others whose names were in the Book of Life, but he was obviously concerned about who was controlling their lives. Since Paul believed that carnality results in divisions, he was surely thinking as he wrote to the Philippians that either Euodias or Syntyche—or both of them—had become carnal.

What a sobering reminder it is that we whose names are in the Book of Life and who have worked closely together can harm our personal relationships and hinder the work of Christ whenever we live for self rather than for Christ.

"Rejoice in the Lord"

Paul then gave a command to all the believers in Philippi: "Rejoice in the Lord alway: and again I say, Rejoice" (Phil. 4:4, KJV). It is not only a privilege to rejoice in the Lord—it is a command.

It would have been one thing if Paul had emphasized occasional rejoicing, but he used the tense for the word "rejoice" which emphasized continual rejoicing. And—as if that were not enough—he said "alway," or "at all times."

And since people forget so easily, he added, "And again I say, Rejoice."

Notice the sphere in which one is to rejoice—"in the Lord." This means that the individual believer must be convinced that the Lord knows what He is doing and that He makes no mistakes. Even though we do not understand our circumstances, we can have complete confidence in God to use the circumstances for our good and for His glory.

When Job was enduring his severe test and even his friends were accusing him of wrong doing, he triumphantly declared, "But He knows the way I take; when He has tried me, I shall come forth as gold" (Job 23:10). Job was rejoicing in the Lord in spite of his trials, and he was able to do that because he had unquestioned confidence in God.

The psalmist revealed the same kind of confidence: "O Lord, Thou hast searched me and known me. Thou dost know when I sit down and when I rise up; Thou dost understand my thought from afar. Thou dost scrutinize my path and my lying down, and art intimately acquainted with all my ways. Even before there is a word on my tongue, behold, O Lord, Thou dost know it all. Thou hast enclosed me behind and before, and laid Thy hand upon me. Such knowledge is too wonderful for me; it is too high, I cannot attain to it" (Ps. 139:1-6).

In the New Testament, James said, "Blessed is a man who perseveres under trial; for once he has been approved, he will receive the crown of life, which the Lord has promised to those who love Him" (James 1:12). So when we accept trials with the proper attitude, a crown of life awaits us.

At times the trials can be severe, and the Christians undergoing them may wonder if they will be able to hold up under them. However, the Word of God promises, "No temptation has overtaken you but such as is common to man; and God is faithful, who will not allow you to be tempted beyond what you are able, but with the temptation will provide the way of escape also, that you may be able to endure it" (I Cor. 10:13).

Rejoicing, or joy, is part of the fruit of the Spirit (see Gal. 5:22). Therefore, it is not something that a person works up on his own; it is produced in him as he has a right relationship with and attitude toward, the indwelling Holy Spirit.

True joy affects the emotions, but expression of the emotions is not necessarily rejoicing. Joy usually brings happiness, but happiness is not necessarily joy. Happiness usually depends on happenings, but joy depends on the Holy Spirit within us. Joy is based on our knowledge of Christ, especially our knowledge of who He is and what He is to us. And how wonderful it is that nothing can separate us from His love, which includes His purpose and determination to shower us with all kinds of benefits (see Rom. 8:35-39). That's something to rejoice about! We can rejoice in Him always.

According to Ephesians 1:3, God "has blessed us with every spiritual blessing in the heavenly places in Christ." No one can ever diminish what God has already done for us. This certainly gives us something to rejoice about regardless of the circumstances through which we are passing at the present time. Perhaps your feelings are not sufficient at the present to cause you to rejoice, but rejoicing in what God has already done for you will produce a positive change of attitude. So if you cannot rejoice in your circumstances, rejoice in the Lord. If you cannot rejoice in your friends, rejoice in the Lord. Even if you cannot rejoice in yourself, rejoice in the Lord.

Because we have bodies of flesh, we are subject to change and fluctuation, but it is wonderful to rejoice in God, who is above change and fluctuation. Malachi 3:6 says, "For I, the Lord, do not change." Numbers 23:19 says, "God is not a man, that He should lie, nor a son of man, that He should repent; has He said, and will He not do it? Or has He spoken, and will He not make it good?" James 1:17 says, "Every good thing bestowed and every perfect gift is from above, coming down from the Father of lights, with whom there is no variation, or shifting shadow."

So regardless of our circumstances, let us rejoice in the Lord always, as Paul commanded the believers in Philippi. This is a righteous command which believers are expected to obey. And it can be obeyed because it is a matter of the will and is based on the work of the Holy Spirit in us and on our faith in His love for us.

During those times when you are down and it seems very difficult to rejoice, I encourage you to read Psalm 37 and let your heart be refreshed by the Lord. The entire psalm is

wonderful, but especially notice verses 1-6: "Fret not yourself
because of evildoers, be not envious toward wrongdoers. For
they will wither quickly like the grass, and fade like the
green herb. Trust in the Lord, and do good; dwell in the land
and cultivate faithfulness. Delight yourself in the Lord; and
He will give you the desires of your heart. Commit your way
to the Lord, trust also in Him, and He will do it. And He will
bring forth your righteousness as the light, and your judgment as the noonday."

So in spite of the past we can start praising God because
we believe in Him. And we will be helped to rejoice as we keep
going to the Word to have our hearts encouraged concerning
all He has done for us and is even now doing in us.

Returning to Philippians 4, note again the three admoni-
tions which are "in the Lord." Paul commanded believers to
"stand fast in the Lord" (v. 1, KJV) because He is in our
midst. Paul commanded them to "be of the same mind in the
Lord" (v. 2, KJV) because we possess His mind and need to
practice unity. And Paul also commanded, "Rejoice in the
Lord alway" (v. 4, KJV) because He does not change and has
only our best interests in His heart and mind.

God's Provision for Peace

Philippians 4:5-7 reveals God's sufficient provision for our
peace: "Let your moderation be known unto all men. The
Lord is at hand. Be careful for nothing; but in every thing by
prayer and supplication with thanksgiving let your requests
be made known unto God. And the peace of God, which
passeth all understanding, shall keep your hearts and minds
through Christ Jesus" (KJV).

It is important to notice the distinction between peace *with*
God and the peace *of* God. Romans 5:1 emphasizes peace
with God: "Therefore having been justified by faith, we have
peace with God through our Lord Jesus Christ." When the
believer is brought into right relationship with God through
faith in Jesus Christ, he is declared righteous before God, so
he has peace *with* God. However, many people who have
trusted Jesus Christ as Saviour and have peace with God do
not have the peace of God.

Ephesians 2:14 refers to the peace of God: "For He Himself

is our peace." The peace of God is also referred to in Colossians 3:15: "Let the peace of Christ rule in your hearts." It was the peace of God Jesus was concerned about when He said, "Peace I leave with you; My peace I give to you; not as the world gives, do I give to you. Let not your heart be troubled, nor let it be fearful" (John 14:27). In the same regard, Jesus said, "These things have I spoken to you, that in Me you may have peace. In the world you have tribulation, but take courage; I have overcome the world" (16:33).

Salvation in Christ

In Philippians 4:5-7 the subject is specifically the peace *of* God; that is, it is the way to peace of heart. Peace is probably man's greatest desire. The lost and condemned seek it; the bewildered believer seeks it. It is the height and depth of man's heart search everywhere. Peace is not some religious article; it is not some thing off by itself. Peace is associated with a Person—Jesus Christ. It is not something to be achieved; it is something to be received. It is not a work, it is a fruit. And one cannot have the fruit without the root—he must be rightly related to Jesus Christ. Peace is part of the fruit of the Spirit (see Gal. 5:22).

There is no formula for peace. If someone could produce such a formula, he would win undying fame. And if it could be sold, he could become the world's richest person because people everywhere are seeking peace. But it cannot be done this way. The beginning of this peace is in Christ and His Person. It is received as a result of meeting certain conditions in conjunction with one's receiving Jesus Christ. This peace is related both to the Person and the work of Jesus Christ.

Verses 5 and 6 of Philippians 4 outline the conditions for receiving the peace of God: "Let your moderation be known unto all men. The Lord is at hand. Be careful for nothing; but in every thing by prayer and supplication with thanksgiving let your requests be made known unto God" (KJV).

It is understood that the person Paul was addressing had already accepted God's provision for peace *with* God; that is, he had already trusted Jesus Christ as his personal Saviour. In so doing, he had obtained peace through the shed blood of

Christ. Colossians 1:20 says of Christ, "And through Him to reconcile all things to Himself, having made peace through the blood of His cross." The person who trusts Jesus Christ as personal Saviour becomes "justified by faith" and has "peace with God through our Lord Jesus Christ" (Rom. 5:1). The results that follow are seen in the next verse: "Through whom also we have obtained our introduction by faith into this grace in which we stand; and exult in hope of the glory of God" (v. 2). So regarding conditions for experiencing the personal peace of God, salvation itself is assumed as the first condition.

Moderation

Through Paul's words to the Philippians we see what other conditions are involved. First, he said, "Let your moderation be known unto all men" (Phil. 4:5, KJV). The Greek word translated "moderation" has many shades of meaning. It can mean "bigheartedness, forbearance, kindliness, reasonableness, consideration, charitableness, generosity." In a sense, this one word incorporates the whole fruit of the Spirit, as mentioned in Galatians 5:22,23. The Amplified Bible translates Philippians 4:5: "Let all men know and perceive and recognize your unselfishness—your considerateness, your forbearing spirit. The Lord is near—He is coming soon."

Notice that we are not just to possess moderation; we are to express it—"Let your moderation be known unto all men" (v. 5, KJV). The "all men" would include both saved and unsaved. Each believer is to be a good witness and to let the indwelling Christ reveal Himself in and through the believer so that others may observe the Christ-life. Paul urged us to live in such a way because "the Lord is at hand" (v. 5, KJV). Not only might He come at any time, but also He is in us right now to strengthen us to accomplish all of this.

The word "moderation" (v. 5) emphasizes pliability and agreeableness. It is a special consideration given to other people, and it is to be the additive that causes a believer to patiently forbear under injury without desiring revenge. It is a spirit that is ready to forgive, and it possesses a gentleness of temper. It is also temperate in physical desires and demonstrates equity; that is, justice and impartiality in business.

Having moderation means a person will avoid extremes and will not be explosive. The peace of God is obviously not in a person's life if he has an explosive temper. Nor can there be peace in a stubborn heart that refuses to yield to reason or to God. Nor is there the peace of God for the one living in physical excess; this only breeds greed and discontent.

It cannot be overemphasized that the "moderation" of which Paul spoke in Philippians 4:5 is related to the indwelling Holy Spirit and the fruit that is produced by Him in our lives. That is why Paul used the word "let" in saying, "Let your moderation be known" (v. 5, KJV). We cannot self-produce moderation any more than we can self-produce the mind of Christ. Since Christ indwells us, we are to "let this mind be in [us], which was also in Christ Jesus" (2:5, KJV). So also, since the Holy Spirit indwells us, we are to let Him do His work in our lives to produce His fruit through us. And we are enabled to do this because "the Lord is at hand" (4:5, KJV).

"Be Careful for Nothing"

The next condition Paul mentioned for personal peace is to "be careful for nothing" (Phil. 4:6, KJV). The Amplified Bible translates this phrase: "Do not fret or have any anxiety about anything."

Although this is a negative command, it is followed by a positive one: "But in every thing by prayer and supplication with thanksgiving let your requests be made known unto God" (v. 6, KJV).

Care and prayer are as mutually opposed as fire and water. Paul was not referring to being unconcerned when he said, "Be careful for nothing" (v. 6, KJV). The word translated "be careful for" means "to be anxious" or "to be troubled with cares." From the context it is apparent that Paul was trying to help believers so they would not always be worrying about the future.

It is not wrong to have a genuine concern for others, especially for their needs. Galatians 6:2 says, "Bear one another's burdens, and thus fulfill the law of Christ." We are to concern ourselves with the needs of others, but we are not to be obsessed with what might happen in the future. It is understandable that Christians become anxious concerning the future from exposure to the news media. But they must leave the future to God. He is still on the throne, and He can work out His plan in the future even as He has in the past and present.

If we permit ourselves, we can become extremely anxious about the future as we look at what is happening in world governments. We see and experience a declining economy, and enemies seek to outdistance us in the arms race. The individual believer can do very little about all of this. So each of us must remind ourselves that we need to be more concerned about God and His will than about the uncertainties of the future. We need to get our eyes off our personal anxieties and the sources of our distresses and to focus them on God, who is the source of our peace. This is the only way we can obtain peace because peace does not come from what happens around us; it comes only from God, who is the Prince of Peace.

There are at least three characteristics, or marks, that indicate we have excessive care. The first is being more concerned about things than about God's will for us. We will never have peace by acquiring things; peace comes only by being in God's will, with or without the possessions we think we so greatly need. Ours in the western world is a credit card society, and we are able to obtain about anything we want almost instantly. Then the anxiety comes in struggling to pay for all that was bought on impulse. Whether anxiety comes from wanting possessions or from concern over how to pay for them, it must be underscored that anxiety chokes the life of faith and strangles the peace of God. Anxiety yields only worry. Someone has said, "Worry is the interest we pay on the debt of unbelief with which we have mortgaged our life."

A second mark of excessive care is that in our hurried state we allow ourselves to be pressured into hasty decisions and actions. Life provides many illustrations of times when we feel we must make a decision immediately, and then later we realize it was not that urgent after all. When we are in league with God, we can afford to wait for His perfect time.

The psalmist had a great deal to say about waiting on the

Lord. He said, "Wait for the Lord; be strong, and let your
heart take courage; yes, wait for the Lord" (Ps. 27:14). He
also said, "Rest in the Lord and wait patiently for Him"
(37:7), and, "Wait for the Lord, and keep His way" (v. 34).

A third characteristic of excessive care is that we are constantly agitated because of unrest in our souls. Faith—not
worry—brings answers to prayers. But someone may ask,
"How can one who has so many troubles and problems be
without care or anxiety? He cannot just ignore them, can
he?" The answer is seen by noting what Paul said in Philippians 4:6. He did not stop with the statement, "Be careful for
nothing" (KJV). He went on to say, "But in every thing by
prayer and supplication with thanksgiving let your requests
be made known unto God"(KJV). In other words, don't be
fearful, be prayerful. This is not ignoring the problems;
instead, it is bringing God into our problems by prayer—and
this is the only way to find solutions to the problems.

Remember the statement of verse 5: "The Lord is at hand"
(KJV). God is there, and He has a cure for every care. He
wants us to bring our cares to Him. Peter instructed believers, "Casting all your anxiety upon Him, because He cares
for you" (I Pet. 5:7). This includes not just a few of the cares,
but all of them; not just the big problems, but the little ones
too. Some people have what I call "pet cares." They like to
keep these cares to talk about, and one gets the feeling they
do not really want to get rid of them. But God says we are to
bring *all* of our cares to Him. Usually one discovers he is
either casting all of his cares upon God, or he is keeping all of
his cares for himself. It is difficult to go halfway in this
matter. But every care we commit to God is met by His love
and power. As someone said, "Our 'all care' is met by His 'all
power.' "

The Bible tells us, "Cast your burden upon the Lord, and
He will sustain you; He will never allow the righteous to be
shaken" (Ps. 55:22). Our cares are to be cast on the Lord, as
indicated by Psalm 37:5: "Commit your way to the Lord,
trust also in Him, and He will do it."

Consider also the fact that God has a cure for care. This is
seen in Matthew 6:25-34. Having told of the way God cares
for even the birds, Jesus said, "Therefore do not be anxious
for tomorrow; for tomorrow will care for itself. Each day has

enough trouble of its own" (v. 34). God's cure for care is seen specifically in verse 33: "Seek first His kingdom and His righteousness; and all these things shall be added to you." Meditate on this passage of Scripture and let it be an encouragement to your heart.

Hebrews 12:2 instructs us to be "looking unto Jesus the author and finisher of our faith"(KJV). The writer was here actually emphasizing "looking away unto Jesus." We are to look away from the things that worry us and look to Him. We are to look to Him in whom there is no worry whatsoever.

Isaiah 26:3,4 says, "The steadfast of mind Thou wilt keep in perfect peace, because he trusts in Thee. Trust in the Lord forever, for in God the Lord, we have an everlasting Rock." We have already frequently cited verses in Psalm 37 in this regard. Notice especially verses 1-7. And remember also Jesus' words: "In Me you may have peace" (John 16:33).

Prescription for Prayer

Paul did not want the Philippian believers to be anxious for anything; instead, he wanted them to make their needs known to God by means of prayer, supplication and requests. Philippians 4:6 gives a prescription for prayer, and this prescription has three elements. If we wish to be successful in our prayer life, we cannot omit any element. It is not our right to decide to omit any element any more than the pharmacist has the liberty to leave out an element of a prescription written by a doctor.

Notice the three words in Philippians 4:6 that relate to prayer. The first one, which is translated "prayer," is a common word for prayer and always refers to prayer addressed to God. This includes addressing God in worship and adoration, such as was done by the psalmist.

The word translated "supplication" emphasizes a sense of need—even desperate personal needs. The word is used of requests made by one person of another as well as to people's requesting things from God.

The third word is translated "requests" and refers to something asked for or to a petition. This is usually something very specific.

The three words seem to move from the general to the

particular. They emphasize the importance of believers' being specific in their prayers.

Prayer is a particular exercise with a specific objective. In other words, start with prayer, adoration, worship and supplication, and then state your particular requests. It is not that we pray to give God information for His sake—He knows about it already. But we should pray as though we are giving Him all this information and as though He needed it. Be sincere about it. This stimulates faith and expectation.

Remember, when we pray, we pray to God, not to ourselves. The Scriptures tell of two men, a Pharisee and a publican, or tax gatherer, who went into the temple to pray (see Luke 18:10-14). Because the Pharisee was self-righteous and considered himself above the lowly tax gatherer, the Scriptures state that the Pharisee "was praying thus to himself" (v. 11). God does not hear the prayers of a self-righteous person—he prays only to himself. So as you come to God, make your requests known to Him. Depend on Him for solutions, and then your prayers will not be to yourself but to God.

With Thanksgiving

Notice that all the aspects of prayer in Philippians 4:6 are to be made "with thanksgiving" (KJV). This is extremely important. In fact, I would say these are the most important words in this passage.

Frequently I hear those leading in public prayer say at the end of their prayer, "And we will praise Thee for it." Usually this refers to having prayed for something specific with the intention that, when God answers the prayer, they will praise Him for it. There is nothing wrong with such an expression, although it is a shame that we so often forget to later praise God for the answered prayer. But Paul was concerned that thanksgiving be offered with the prayer, not waiting until some later time when the answer is experienced. Even while praying for the need, we are to thank God for His answer. This, of course, takes faith that God will answer, so it is a test of whether or not one really believes God. To be able to give thanks even before one has the answer is an important sign of faith in the believer's life.

With Faith

This brings us to the question, What is faith? The Scriptures give their own definition: "Now faith is the substance of things hoped for, the evidence of things not seen" (Heb. 11:1, KJV). The Amplified Bible renders this verse: "Now faith is the assurance (the confirmation, the title-deed) of the things [we] hope for, being the proof of things [we] do not see and the conviction of their reality—faith perceiving as real fact what is not revealed to the senses."

Hebrews 11 gives several examples of those who lived a life of faith. Concerning Noah it is said, "By faith Noah, being warned by God about things not yet seen, in reverence prepared an ark for the salvation of his household, by which he condemned the world, and became an heir of the righteousness which is according to faith" (v. 7). Even though it had never rained before Noah's time, Noah took God at His word that a flood was coming and built an ark to save his family.

Concerning Abraham it is said, "By faith Abraham, when he was called, obeyed by going out to a place which he was to receive for an inheritance; and he went out, not knowing where he was going" (v. 8). Concerning Moses it is said, "By faith he left Egypt, not fearing the wrath of the king; for he endured, as seeing Him who is unseen" (v. 27).

So faith is really thanking God for the answer to what we have just prayed. In effect, it is saying, "God, since I am expecting to get what I asked for, I thank you for it now."

Jesus Himself said, "If any man is thirsty, let him come to Me and drink. He who believes in Me, as the Scripture said, 'From his innermost being shall flow rivers of living water'" (John 7:37,38). One is not left wondering what Jesus was referring to. The Scriptures add, "But this He spoke of the Spirit, whom those who believed in Him were to receive, for the Spirit was not yet given, because Jesus was not yet glorified" (v. 39).

Coming and drinking are equivalent to praying and taking the answer by thanking the Lord for it. It is a coming to Him and taking what He has to offer. So we can thank Him for the answer even as we pray concerning the need.

Many keep praying and asking and then wonder why there is no answer. One reason may be that they have not shown that they believe God really will answer. If they had such faith, they would thank God for the answer, even at the time of prayer. The Bible says, "Watch and pray" (Matt. 26:41, KJV), not "Pray and wonder if He will answer." We are to watch Him answer.

Thankful praying is not wishful praying. We would hardly thank God for something we are only wishing for, but if we are convinced that it is God's will to answer, it shows faith and expectancy of heart to thank Him for the answer even when we pray for it.

A principle of believing prayer is seen in Mark 11:22-24: "And Jesus answered saying to them, 'Have faith in God. Truly I say to you, whoever says to this mountain, "Be taken up and cast into the sea," and does not doubt in his heart, but believes that what he says is going to happen; it shall be granted him. Therefore I say to you, all things for which you pray and ask, believe that you have received them, and they shall be granted you.' " Prayer is not only asking, but a prayer based on His Word is also saying, as here mentioned.

Consider also what prayer and supplication, with thanksgiving, does to worry and fretting. One cannot pray with thanksgiving while fretting and worrying. Thanksgiving and fretting are at opposite poles.

Let me especially encourage you to consider Psalm 103: "Bless the Lord, O my soul; and all that is within me, bless His holy name. Bless the Lord, O my soul, and forget none of His benefits; who pardons all your iniquities; who heals all your diseases; who redeems your life from the pit; who crowns you with lovingkindness and compassion; who satisfies your years with good things, so that your youth is renewed like the eagle" (vv. 1-5).

Consider also Psalm 34, especially verses 1-3: "I will bless the Lord at all times; His praise shall continually be in my mouth. My soul shall make its boast in the Lord; the humble shall hear it and rejoice. O magnify the Lord with me, and let us exalt His name together." Both of these psalms are tremendous food for thought, and I encourage you to meditate on them in your devotional time, letting the Lord minister to your heart through them.

If we fail to thank God both for what He has done and for what He says He will do, why should He do any more? There is no need for Him to do any more because we are really not believing Him. And no one needs to wonder whether or not it is God's will for him to give thanks. The Bible says, "In everything give thanks; for this is God's will for you in Christ Jesus" (I Thess. 5:18).

Elements of the Peace of God

In writing to the believers in Philippi, Paul gave them the conditions that must be met in order to have the peace of God (Phil. 4:5,6). Paul then told them the result they could expect: "And the peace of God, which passeth all understanding, shall keep your hearts and minds through Christ Jesus" (v. 7, KJV).

From verse 7 we see three elements, or qualities, of this peace. First, it is the peace of God. Second, it is a peace which passes all understanding. Third, it is a peace that keeps one's heart and mind through Christ Jesus. Let us consider these in detail.

Of God

First, it is the peace of God. It is not a psychological effect; it does not spring from the mind as its source. The peace to which Paul referred does not arise out of events or circumstances. The source of this peace is none other than God Himself. This is why Colossians 3:15 says, "Let the peace of Christ rule in your hearts."

Many people run to psychologists and psychiatrists today for answers to their disturbed minds. We praise God for Christian psychologists and psychiatrists who really understand the spiritual principles, but the majority of psychologists and psychiatrists are unsaved individuals who use the standards of the world and give no consideration to the Word of God. These psychiatrists and psychologists probe the people who come to them for the cause of their problems and seek whom to blame or what to blame. And even when the real cause surfaces—the sin problem—it is sometimes explained away as psychological in nature or a false sensitivity produced by childhood training. However, the way to peace of heart is only through Jesus Christ. Not only does He give us His peace (see John 14:27; 16:33), He is our peace (see Eph. 2:14).

Beyond Understanding

A second quality of the peace mentioned by Paul in Philippians 4:7 is that it goes beyond understanding—"which passeth all understanding" (KJV).

It is the type of peace that sometimes defies all logic. Even believers cannot explain it, and unbelievers cannot explain it away, for it is not possible to analyze this kind of peace. Even so, one can certainly enjoy it. It is beyond the reach of the mind but within the realm of Christian experience.

There is much emphasis today on experience, and it is often erroneous because some even want to determine doctrine by experience. But Philippians 4:7 is a verse of experience as it tells of the peace of God that goes beyond all comprehension. This is an experience that will produce deep-seated joy in the heart of every individual who has it.

Jesus was the perfect example of such peace. Once when He was in a boat with His disciples, there arose such a violent storm that even the boat was covered with waves. But Jesus Himself was asleep. The account of this incident is recorded in Matthew 8:23-27. The frantic disciples awoke Jesus and exclaimed, "Save us, Lord; we are perishing!" (v. 25). Notice His response: "He said to them, 'Why are you timid, you men of little faith?' Then He arose, and rebuked the wind and the sea; and it became perfectly calm" (v. 26). This same Jesus indwells us to give us the kind of peace He had at that time.

Knowing that it is this kind of peace that is referred to, it is even more thrilling to read: "Peace I leave with you; My peace I give to you; not as the world gives, do I give to you. Let not your heart be troubled, nor let it be fearful" (John 14:27). In the first verse of this same chapter Jesus told the disciples: "Let not your heart be troubled; believe in God, believe also in Me."

To Guard Us

The third quality of the peace mentioned by Paul in Philippians 4:7 is that it "shall keep your hearts and minds through Christ Jesus" (KJV). It is a keeping peace. The Greek word translated "shall keep" was a common word in the days of the Roman Empire. It referred to protecting by guarding. The Philippians would have been familiar with the Roman soldiers who stood guard at various important places in the empire. Those within a guarded building did not need to worry about what was on the outside as long as the Roman soldiers were there. So, too, the heart that has the peace of God does not need to worry about what might happen.

From this we see that the peace of God is not merely a feeling that we are to keep, it is a particular quality of peace that keeps, or guards, us. It keeps us in times of trouble, trial and turmoil. And it is this same peace that Jesus left with believers when He went to be with the Father (see John 14:27).

The peace of God is sent by God to do sentry duty, to guard our hearts and minds. This involves our thinking and the emotions that result from our thinking. The peace of God guards against threatening intrusions of all kinds.

The peace of God is quite different from what many people imagine. It does not mean that we will escape the battle of life and the persecution which results from it. Even though I am convinced the Scriptures teach that God will rapture the Church before the seven-year period of the Tribulation begins, God has not promised before then to deliver Christians from all persecution. The believers in Philippi surely had undergone persecution, and the believers in Thessalonica had certainly experienced many trials. So just because we have the peace of God does not mean we will not undergo severe testings and persecution in this world.

Neither does having the peace of God mean what David once expressed: "O that I had wings like a dove! I would fly away and be at rest" (Ps. 55:6). One must remember that before that statement, he said, "My heart is in anguish within me, and the terrors of death have fallen upon me. Fear and trembling come upon me; and horror has overwhelmed me" (vv. 4,5). Later, David cried out, "As for me, I shall call upon God, and the Lord will save me. Evening and morning and at noon, I will complain and murmur, and He will hear my voice. He will redeem my soul in peace from the battle which is against me" (vv. 16-18). No wonder David said, "Cast your burden upon the Lord, and He will sustain you; He will never allow the righteous to be shaken" (v. 22). So even though we may sometimes want to fly away from all our troubles, we must come to our spiritual senses as did David and realize that God can sustain us even in the midst of troubles.

Specific troubles may be so intense that a person is even physically afraid. That is the time to be encouraged by David's statement: "When I am afraid, I will put my trust in Thee. In God, whose word I praise, in God I have put my trust; I shall not be afraid. What can mere man do to me?" (Ps. 56:3,4). David echoed the same thoughts in verses 11-13: "In God I have put my trust, I shall not be afraid. What can man do to me? Thy vows are binding upon me, O God; I will render thank offerings to Thee. For Thou hast delivered my soul from death, indeed my feet from stumbling, so that I may walk before God in the light of the living."

It is also important to remember that the peace of God mentioned in Philippians 4:7 is not a promise of exemption from troubles, difficulties and disappointments of life. Remember, the same apostle who wrote Philippians 4:7 also wrote II Corinthians 11:23-33, in which he told what he had endured for the cause of Christ. Consider especially what he said in verses 23-27: "Are they servants of Christ? (I speak as if insane) I more so; in far more labors, in far more imprisonments, beaten times without number, often in danger of death. Five times I received from the Jews thirty-nine lashes. Three times I was beaten with rods, once I was stoned, three times I was shipwrecked, a night and a day I have spent in the deep. I have been on frequent journeys, in dangers from rivers, dangers from robbers, dangers from my countrymen, dangers from the Gentiles, dangers in the city, dangers in the wilderness, dangers on the sea, dangers among false brethren; I have been in labor and hardship, through many sleepless nights, in hunger and thirst, often without food, in cold and exposure."

Yet Paul learned a valuable lesson in the midst of all of his difficulties which led him to say, "Therefore I am well content with weaknesses, with insults, with distresses, with persecutions, with difficulties, for Christ's sake; for when I am weak, then I am strong" (12:10). No doubt it was experiences like these that caused Paul to be able to write that the peace of God goes beyond all human comprehension (Phil. 4:7).

Paul did not say that in return for having accomplished what is stated in Philippians 4:5,6 we shall receive preferred treatment and be exempt from the troubles of life. However, Paul was wishing for the believers in Philippi—and for us—to grasp the glorious truth that when troubles come, our souls will stand unassailable against the onslaughts because God Himself will protect us. The God of peace will guard the door to our hearts.

When we come to the realization of this truth, we will be able to say with the psalmist, "What can mere man do to me?" (Ps. 56:4). We will also be able to say: "From my distress I called upon the Lord; the Lord answered me and set me in a large place. The Lord is for me; I will not fear; what can man do to me?" (118:5,6). How wonderful it is to experience the promise of Christ: "I will never desert you, nor will I ever forsake you" (Heb. 13:5). This allows us to say with the writer of Hebrews, "So that we confidently say, 'The Lord is my helper, I will not be afraid. What shall man do to me?'" (v. 6).

Paul said that God's peace guards our hearts and minds through Christ Jesus (Phil. 4:7). The ultimate secret of this peace that defends the soul is Jesus Christ Himself, not some psychological peace. Jesus has not only given us this peace (John 14:27), but He is our peace (Eph. 2:14). When we fulfill the conditions of Philippians 4:5,6, we will experience the results of verse 7.

The words of the song "Peace, Perfect Peace" have been especially encouraging to me over the years. Think carefully of these words and consider the message the next time you sing it:

> Peace, perfect peace, in this dark world of sin?
> The blood of Jesus whispers peace within.

Peace, perfect peace, by thronging duties pressed?
To do the will of Jesus, this is rest.

Peace, perfect peace with sorrows surging round?
On Jesus' bosom naught but calm is found.

Peace, perfect peace, our future all unknown?
Jesus we know, and He is on the throne.

Peace, perfect peace, death shadowing us and ours?
Jesus has vanquished death and all its powers.

It is enough: earth's struggles soon shall cease,
And Jesus, call us to heav'n's perfect peace.

—Edward H. Bickersteth

Chapter 8

Christ Our Strength (cont.)

As Paul neared the end of his letter to the believers at Philippi, he wrote some especially important and practical advice.

Provision for Our Thought Life

Paul told the Philippian believers—and by inspiration it applies to us—"Finally, brethren, whatsoever things are true, whatsoever things are honest, whatsoever things are just, whatsoever things are pure, whatsoever things are lovely, whatsoever things are of good report; if there be any virtue, and if there be any praise, think on these things" (Phil. 4:8, KJV). This verse reveals God's sufficient provision for our thought life.

Importance of Our Thoughts

I used to receive a business magazine which had only one word on the cover—*Think*. The artwork on the cover was usually beautifully done, but it was that one word that especially intrigued me. Someone has suggested that 85 percent of the people don't think, 10 percent of the people think they think, and only 5 percent of the people think! There is no way of knowing the exact percentage, but this statement pointedly hits home at an obvious truth.

The thought life of every believer is very important, but the question that often arises is, How can I control my thoughts? It is important to recognize from the outset that it is possible to control our thoughts. Paul wrote, "For the weapons of our

156

warfare are not of the flesh, but divinely powerful for the destruction of fortresses. We are destroying speculations and every lofty thing raised up against the knowledge of God, and we are taking every thought captive to the obedience of Christ" (II Cor. 10:4,5).

When thoughts enter our minds that are not pleasing to the Lord, we must use the weapons we have available by relying on the Lord to enable us to overcome the bad thoughts. At such times, we need to say something like this: "God, I realize that thought is not pleasing to You. Take care of it—captivate it—so my thoughts will be honoring to You." When we mean business, God always answers.

It is interesting to see where Paul's exhortation about their thought life came in the progression of his instructions to the Philippians. First, Paul said, "Stand fast in the Lord" (Phil. 4:1, KJV). Second, he said, "Be of the same mind in the Lord" (v. 2, KJV). Third, he said, "Rejoice in the Lord" (v. 4, KJV). Fourth, he said, "Let your requests be made known unto God" (v. 6, KJV). Fifth, he said, "The peace of God . . . shall keep your hearts and minds" (v. 7, KJV). Sixth, he said, "Think on these things" (v. 8, KJV). Seventh, he said, "Those things, . . . do: . . . and the God of peace shall be with you" (v. 9, KJV). The progression is from prayer, to peace, to thinking, to doing.

Paul gave many practical exhortations to the believers in Philippi, one of the most important of which was what to think about. Paul realized that what a person thinks about characterizes what he really is. King Solomon was the wisest person until Jesus Christ came, and Solomon said of man, "For as he thinks within himself, so is he" (Prov. 23:7). We are a direct product of our thinking, so it is exceedingly important to control what we think about. The New Testament urges believers, "If then you have been raised up with Christ, keep seeking the things above, where Christ is, seated at the right hand of God. Set your mind on the things above, not on the things that are on the earth. For you have died and your life is hidden with Christ in God" (Col. 3:1-3).

Our thoughts are the seeds that produce the deeds. This is why Paul, after having told the Philippians what to think about (Phil. 4:8), told them to do those things (v. 9). One cannot have proper actions unless he is characterized by wholesome thinking. Some Christians are the victims of wrong thoughts, but remember, when we have met the conditions, the peace of God guards our minds (v. 7).

A good exercise is to analyze the kind of thoughts you have been thinking. Some will be spiritual thoughts which make a positive contribution to life, others will be thoughts about things that are not necessarily good or bad, and there will be thoughts that are definitely bad—and you realize this without anyone's telling you so. The quickest way to deteriorate or to degenerate is to allow your mind to be occupied with unworthy thoughts. We soon become what we think. Thinking good thoughts contributes to building character; thinking bad thoughts leads downward.

Romans 1 tells of the downward path taken by those who reject God. It is interesting to note the place that thoughts have in that path. Verse 21 says, "For even though they knew God, they did not honor Him as God, or give thanks; but they became futile in their speculations, and their foolish heart was darkened." Their minds, or thoughts, were involved in knowing God, but their minds were also involved in failing to honor Him and were especially involved in "speculations." They refused to retain God in their thoughts, and they became futile in their thinking, which resulted in foolish reasoning, which in turn led to stupid speculations. "Professing to be wise, they became fools" (v. 22).

What a tragic path people go down who reject God! The end result is that God gives them over to thinking their depraved thoughts: "And just as they did not see fit to acknowledge God any longer, God gave them over to a depraved mind, to do those things which are not proper" (v. 28). Such people become degenerated beyond description, and their thought life is a primary contributing factor in their downward path.

Jesus explained that the mouth really reveals what is in the heart: "The good man out of the good treasure of his heart brings forth what is good; and the evil man out of the evil treasure brings forth what is evil; for his mouth speaks from that which fills his heart" (Luke 6:45). What the conscious mind thinks on gradually sinks into the subconscious mind and becomes the building blocks, or material, for one's character. "For as he thinks within himself, so he is" (Prov. 23:7).

We can make a positive contribution to our subconscious mind by controlling the thoughts of our conscious mind. But when we think selfishly, covetously, jealously and lustfully, these characteristics will become evident in our character.

Even though it may be difficult to do so, we all need to be reminded that it is possible for us to control our thoughts. If it were not possible, we would never be enjoined by the Scriptures to take "every thought captive to the obedience of Christ" (II Cor. 10:5). It is important that each believer bring his thought life into total subjection to Jesus Christ.

Qualities of Our Thoughts

In Philippians 4:8 Paul mentioned six qualities and exhorted believers to think on those things that have those qualities. These really serve as a summary of proper Christian thought life. Paul said, "Finally, brethren, whatsoever things are true, whatsoever things are honest, whatsoever things are just, whatsoever things are pure, whatsoever things are lovely, whatsoever things are of good report; if there be any virtue, and if there be any praise, think on these things" (v. 8, KJV).

"Whatsoever Things Are True." First, Paul enjoined us to think about those things that are true. The word translated "true" has the sense of that which is factually true in contrast to that which is false. No distinction should be drawn between spiritual truth and secular truth—all truth is God's truth. The believer should think on those things that are true, not on those things that are false.

It is especially true in the spiritual realm that we cannot expect to have the right kind of life unless our thinking is right concerning doctrine and practice. One must know truth before he can practice it. So there should be great emphasis on knowing the proper teaching of the Word of God in order that we might live properly. Ephesians 4:14,15 says, "As a result, we are no longer to be children, tossed here and there by waves, and carried about by every wind of doctrine, by the trickery of men, by craftiness in deceitful

scheming; but speaking the truth in love, we are to grow up
in all aspects into Him, who is the head, even Christ."

Paul emphasized the importance of knowing truth when
he said, "That I may know him" (Phil. 3:10, KJV). Paul's
emphasis on truth is also seen in Colossians 3:16: "Let the
word of Christ richly dwell within you; with all wisdom
teaching and admonishing one another with psalms and
hymns and spiritual songs, singing with thankfulness in
your hearts to God."

"Whatsoever Things Are Honest." The second quality
that Paul mentioned is that of honesty: "whatsoever things
are honest" (Phil. 4:8, KJV). The word "honest" is too limited
in meaning today to reveal the full sense of what Paul
intended by the Greek word he used. The Greek word had the
meaning of that which is honorable or worthy of respect. A
Greek scholar who has specialized in word studies suggests
the word combines the elements of gravity and dignity
which invites reverence.

Life today is blighted by lying, perjury and dishonesty in
almost every area—from the lowest level of society to the
highest position. The world is controlled by evil thinking,
not by honest thinking. However, the believer needs to think
on that which is worthy of respect and should have nothing
to do with dishonesty in business, with false advertising or
with the promotion of scandals.

Even though some of these things appeal to the old nature,
we are not to think on them. It is possible to bring every
thought into captivity to Christ. I cannot overemphasize the
importance of making II Corinthians 10:5 part of our spiritual weapons: "Taking every thought captive to the obedience of Christ." By realizing that this is possible, we will be
able to stand more firmly while depending on the Lord to
help us think good thoughts that measure up to Philippians
4:8.

"Whatsoever Things Are Just." A third quality that Paul
mentioned is that a thought should be just: "whatsoever
things are just" (Phil. 4:8, KJV). The word Paul used for
"just" also means "righteous." It refers to that which corre-
sponds to the divine standard.

The tendency is for us to think in the opposite way. We are
quick to pass judgment without hearing both sides of the

issue. We need to exercise caution not only in what we say but also in what we hear. Some things we cannot help hearing; other things we could avoid if we chose to do so. Whatever we hear, we must be sure that we are not gullible in accepting it at face value. We should not pass it on, if there is any doubt in our minds about the truthfulness of the subject matter. Do not forget that the news media or an individual person may get the facts wrong, or at least misinterpret the facts, as the story is passed on. We should not be quick to believe evil about anyone. Perhaps you say, "But Mary told me this, and she never lies." Perhaps that is true, but what she heard may have been a lie, even though she is accurately reporting it.

When someone comes to you and pours out the details of a conflict he or she has had with someone else, do not be quick to take sides with that person until you know more about the situation. A good verse to remember in this case is Proverbs 18:17: "The first to plead his case seems just, until another comes and examines him."

"Whatsoever Things Are Pure." The fourth quality Paul mentioned was that of purity: "whatsoever things are pure" (Phil. 4:8, KJV). The Roman Empire of the first century was morally decadent. It was as bad or worse than the 20th century. Many of the first-century believers were saved out of idol worship which had prostitutes for priestesses, and it was necessary for Paul and other Scripture writers to emphasize the need for purity. When the mind is permitted to drift, it often settles on that which is impure, but believers are to see to it that their minds remain on that which is pure. The Greek word Paul used means "holy" as well as "pure."

Perhaps the quality of purity is one of the most difficult standards to meet for our thought life. We live in a sex-saturated society, and it is extremely difficult to keep one's mind pure. It is extremely important, however, that the Christian have a pure mind. I believe there is a virginity of thought as well as of body. And there certainly can be no chastity of body without the chastity of mind. To think impurely is to live impurely, "for as he thinks within himself, so he is" (Prov. 23:7).

When we discipline our minds to think God's thoughts, we will be thinking on that which is pure. The Bible says, "But the wisdom from above is first pure, then peaceable, gentle, reasonable, full of mercy and good fruits, unwavering, without hypocrisy" (James 3:17).

"Whatsoever Things Are Lovely." The fifth quality Paul mentioned was that of loveliness: "whatsoever things are lovely" (Phil. 4:8, KJV). The word Paul used for "lovely" meant "pleasing" and "agreeable." Believers are to think on that which produces and keeps harmony rather than on that which causes strife. Have you noticed that so many of these characteristics parallel what is said concerning love in I Corinthians 13? As you further consider Philippians 4:8, I would encourage you to read I Corinthians 13 in your devotional time and to meditate on the characteristics of love found there.

"Whatsoever Things Are of Good Report." The sixth quality Paul mentioned was "whatsoever things are of good report" (Phil. 4:8, KJV). This refers to things that are of high quality—elevated truth and principles of all kinds. It is the opposite of bitterness, rancor and evil.

There are so many evil reports today, and if one feeds his mind on these, he will begin to reveal their nature in his character. To feed constantly on negative, rabble-rousing reports does nothing except produce suspicion, jealousy, bitterness and hatred. Even though others may be negative and may purposely slant information, we can determine before God that we will not do so. When we make that determination, God will enable us to carry through on what we have decided.

We need to be especially careful about the way we report spiritual things. Listening to some Christians talk, you would think that no church is doing the work of God that it should be. If you allow yourself to feed on reports that are constantly negative, you will begin to believe what is said and will become less regular in your attendance and less concerned about winning others to Christ and discipling them in the faith.

As we consider reports in the Christian world, let us balance the negative by also looking for the positive that God is doing in places around the world. Some countries that were formerly closed to the gospel or at least gave a great deal of opposition to it, are now much more open to what mission-

aries have to say. Let's be aware that God is still on the
throne and that He will never be without a witness.

As we think on those things that are "of good report" (Phil.
4:8, KJV), we have to eliminate gossip from the list because it
is not of good report. We should be careful what we pass on to
others because what we say may have even a greater effect
than what we intend. Colossians 4:6 admonishes us, "Let
your speech always be with grace, seasoned, as it were, with
salt, so that you may know how you should respond to each
person."

Instead of gossip's being like salt that preserves it is like
poison that destroys. To speak gossip reveals what and how
we think. Gossip deals mostly with scandal and ignores the
injunction to season one's speech with salt. Remember, what
you say betrays what you think, and what you think and say
betrays your character. No wonder Paul emphasized, "Finally, brethren, . . . think on these things" (Phil. 4:8, KJV).

"Those Things . . . Do"

Having emphasized the importance of thinking on the
right kinds of things, Paul told the Philippians, "Those
things, which ye have both learned, and received, and heard,
and seen in me, do: and the God of peace shall be with you"
(Phil. 4:9, KJV).

Notice the four elements in this verse. That which the
Philippians had learned, received, heard and seen in Paul
they were to do. Here we see that thinking is to be properly
counterbalanced by doing. Some seem only to think and not
to do; others primarily do and seem to seldom think. But
after telling the Philippians what to think about, Paul told
them to put it into practice by doing.

The Greek word Paul used for "do" means "to practice." In
addition to the word's inherent meaning of constantly
doing, Paul put it in a Greek tense that would further
emphasize continuous action. Thus, Paul made a double
emphasis on the Philippians' need to constantly demonstrate in their actions all they had learned, received, heard
and seen in him. The doing of verse 9 seems to be related to
the doing of verse 13: "I can do all things through Christ
which strengtheneth me" (KJV).

In the first nine verses of Philippians 4 the order is stand
fast (v. 1), pray (v. 6) and think (v. 8)—all followed by doing
(v. 9).

Some emphasize doing before these other important elements. This is always unwise. However, once the other elements have been considered, one also needs to emphasize the
doing. James said, "To one who knows the right thing to do,
and does not do it, to him it is sin" (James 4:17). What a
convicting verse this is! It assumes first that we know the
right thing to do, which puts the emphasis on thinking and
knowing the truth, or what is right. But once the believer
knows that, he has a tremendous responsibility to follow
through on it or else it becomes a sin to him.

Why is it sin? Because in reality the Christian is renouncing the power of Christ within him when he fails to do what
he knows he should do. If, as a believer, something was
dependent on my power, it would not be a sin; but because
Christ lives in me to accomplish what is right and I refuse to
let Him perform it through me, it is sin.

Jesus said, "If you know these things, you are blessed if
you do them" (John 13:17). Why? Because Jesus lives within
us to do these things. The word "blessed" in John 13:17
actually means "happy." So if we want true happiness, we
will find it through doing those things we know we should.

The God of Peace

Having commanded the Philippians to do those things
which they had learned, received, heard and seen in him,
Paul said, "And the God of peace shall be with you" (Phil.
4:9, KJV). We have distinguished between peace with God
and the peace of God; now we see the God of peace working in
us. Peace is more than a feeling—it is a Person. And that
Person never leaves the believer. Jesus Christ is that Person,
and He has said, "I will never desert you, nor will I ever
forsake you" (Heb. 13:5). This is a very strong statement in
the Greek language. Although double negatives are sub-
standard in English sentence construction, they are frequently used in the Greek language for emphasis. When
Jesus said, "I will never desert you," He used a double negative which could be translated "I will by no means ever

desert you." There is also a double negative in the last phrase: "By no means will I forsake you."

How wonderful it is to have this assurance that the true source of peace will never leave us! Just as we cannot have peace without the Person of Jesus Christ, neither can we have Christ without His peace. Although He lives within us to give us that peace, we need to yield to Him that He might have control of our lives. We have a perfect position in Christ as He indwells us, but we need to appropriate the peace that He provides. Philippians 4:5,6 gives the formula for having the peace of God in one's heart.

Concerning peace, Romans 14:19 says, "Let us pursue the things which make for peace and the building up of one another."

God's Sufficiency for Every Situation

Having instructed the believers in Philippi concerning future spiritual growth, Paul then referred to personal matters. "But I rejoiced in the Lord greatly, that now at the last your care of me hath flourished again; wherein ye were also careful, but ye lacked opportunity. Not that I speak in respect of want: for I have learned, in whatsoever state I am, therewith to be content. I know both how to be abased, and I know how to abound: every where and in all things I am instructed both to be full and to be hungry, both to abound and to suffer need" (Phil. 4:10-12, KJV).

Contentment

From this portion of Paul's letter to the Philippians we see that even Paul had to learn to be content. He was not always that way. And he learned his lesson well because he was able to be content in every situation.

Paul said, "But I rejoiced in the Lord greatly, that now at the last your care of me hath flourished again; wherein ye were also careful, but ye lacked opportunity" (4:10, KJV). Notice that Paul's rejoicing was "in the Lord," not in that which the Philippians had sent to him. Paul rejoiced that the Lord was interested in his need and had used the Philippians to supply that need.

The Lord is interested in every detail of our lives. Matthew 6:31 says, "Do not be anxious then, saying, 'What shall we eat?' or, 'What shall we drink?' or, 'With what shall we clothe ourselves?' " The reasons the believer does not need to be concerned about all of these things are given in the following two verses: "For all these things the Gentiles eagerly seek; for your heavenly Father knows that you need all these things. But seek first His kingdom and His righteousness; and all these things shall be added to you" (vv. 32,33). There can be real contentment as you realize the Lord knows every need you have and that as long as you put Him first, He will supply what you need.

Even though Paul was in confinement as he wrote to the Philippians, he was rejoicing greatly "in the Lord" (Phil. 4:10, KJV). Paul wanted to be sure the Philippians understood that it was not merely their gift he rejoiced over but that he was especially grateful for their thoughtfulness. To explain this, he said, "Not that I am implying that I was in any personal want, for I have learned how to be content (satisfied to the point where I am not disturbed or disquieted) in whatever state I am. I know how to be abased and live humbly in straitened circumstances, and I know also how to enjoy plenty and live in abundance. I have learned in any and all circumstances, the secret of facing every situation, whether well-fed or going hungry, having a sufficiency and to spare or going without and being in want" (vv. 11,12, Amplified).

Another translator renders these verses: "Do not think that I speak thus as having felt the pinch of want. No, I have learned, in whatever condition I am, to be independent of circumstances. I am schooled to bear the depths of poverty, I am schooled to bear abundance. In life as a whole, and in all its circumstances, I have mastered the secret of living—how to be the same amidst repletion and starvation, amidst abundance and privation" (Arthur S. Way).

Notice Paul's words "I have learned" (v. 11, KJV). His ability to adjust to every situation to the point of being content was something he had to learn in his Christian life. Such can result only from a close walk with God while being confident that He makes no mistakes and that the circumstances He is permitting are for our good and His glory.

Notice the word "in" in the phrase "in whatsoever state I am" (v. 11, KJV). Paul was not suggesting—and God was not asking—that we should be content *with* unsatisfactory conditions. But because of our personal relationship with Christ we can be content *in* them. As different situations arise and we learn our lessons one after another, we will also find it possible to be content in every situation.

Contentment is one of those concepts that is easier to define than to experience. This is probably because the tendency is to seek contentment in possessions rather than in a person. We assume that contentment comes from having things, but Paul revealed that it is possible to have deep contentment without things. So often we think contentment would be ours if we were promoted to the next highest position or if we were able to buy that object we think we need so much or if we could be accepted in a certain circle of friends. But as we advance in these areas we discover that contentment is elusive because we are seeking it in the wrong places and in the wrong way.

Contentment does not depend on what we have; it depends on who we are. It is a spiritual attainment, not something that results from purchasing power. As someone has said, "Contentment is a state of heart rather than a statement of account."

Contentment does not necessarily mean satisfaction. In Philippians 3:12-14 Paul stated that he was not satisfied yet with himself but continued to press onward toward the goal. So even though a person is not satisfied with himself or even satisfied with circumstances as they are, he can be content in the situation because of his relationship with the Lord.

Contentment results from the grateful, faithful using of what we have at any given moment. Instead of wishing we had a million dollars, we derive contentment as we faithfully manage the amount of money God has committed to our responsibility. It is not a matter of having our barns full of grain but of having our hearts full of Him.

Learning and Being Instructed

Paul referred to his contentment in two expressions: "I have learned" (Phil. 4:11, KJV) and "I am instructed" (v. 12, KJV).

Paul did not always know contentment, even though he probably came from circumstances of plenty. He did not learn contentment at Gamaliel's feet, where he received theological training. Contentment came by experience under God's hand in all circumstances—even imprisonment. But whether his circumstances included a prison or a pulpit, Paul had learned to be content.

One could cite many people in the Bible to show how God used circumstances to bring them to the place where He wanted them to be. For instance, Joseph was destined for a tremendous task in God's sight, but God took him through 13 years of difficult training before Joseph reached that point. Moses, too, was destined to be a mighty servant of God. God used nearly 80 years in training him for his specific task. David was used mightily of God, but he, too, had to undergo many difficult experiences.

As Paul wrote to the Philippians, he wrote from an atmosphere that could have created great discouragement, yet he could say, "I have learned, in whatsoever state I am, therewith to be content" (v. 11, KJV).

We do not learn contentment while we are murmuring. Old Testament Israel serves as a vivid illustration in this regard. I would encourage you to read the Book of Numbers, which reveals the frequent murmuring of the Israelites even though God had performed so many miracles to take care of them. And even though God occasionally lashed out and judged them severely for their murmuring, they never seemed to learn their lesson. First Corinthians 10 warns us, "Nor grumble, as some of them did, and were destroyed by the destroyer. Now these things happened to them as an example, and they were written for our instruction, upon whom the ends of the ages have come" (vv. 10,11).

The Israelites murmured every time something was not right, and that is often what we do. Some want to explain this away and say, "That's only human." I realize it is human, but Christ Jesus has come to indwell us, and He has given us His peace, which produces contentment, if we will allow Him to have control in our lives.

Paul further explained to the Philippians, "I know both how to be abased, and I know how to abound: every where and in all things I am instructed both to be full and to be hungry, both to abound and to suffer need" (Phil. 4:12, KJV).

Paul had undergone experiences of all extremes that brought him to this point. Some of these experiences can be read about in II Corinthians 11:23-33. He knew what it was to be at the bottom as well as at the top. Yet, he accepted all of this as teaching from the Lord, for he said, "I am instructed" (Phil. 4:12, KJV). He had learned the secret of being content, for he had learned to wait independently of external circumstances. Paul was content because he had learned to depend on Christ.

Although he was apparently reared in the lap of luxury and had known a life of comfort as a young man, Paul had learned to be content because he was instructed in this by the experiences he received from the Lord. It is important that every believer learn what it is to be content because of his relationship with Jesus Christ. The style of life in the western world, however, has produced mostly discontent. Everyone is trying to advance his own position—to have a nicer wardrobe, a nicer car, a nicer house. Someone has said, "Our standard of living is so high that it takes all of our time to produce, and we have no time left to live."

Whereas Paul knew the luxuries of life on the one hand, he also knew the stern, strict and unadorned life of imprisonment. He knew a life of poverty, sickness and sorrow. But through all of these things he had learned to be content and was able to say, "This one thing I do, forgetting those things which are behind, and reaching forth unto those things which are before, I press toward the mark for the prize of the high calling of God in Christ Jesus" (3:13,14, KJV).

We cannot overemphasize that the secret of contentment is not in circumstances that are always changing but is in Jesus Christ who does not change (see Heb. 13:8).

Secret of the Christian's Victorious Life

I believe the key verse of Philippians 4 is verse 13: "I can do all things through Christ which strengtheneth me" (KJV). The Amplified Bible renders this verse: "I have strength for all things in Christ Who empowers me—I am ready for anything and equal to anything through Him Who infuses inner strength into me, [that is, I am self-sufficient in Christ's sufficiency]."

Christ's Sufficiency

Philippians 4:13 is the secret, or key, of the Christian's victorious life. This verse reveals that a believer is self-sufficient in Christ's sufficiency. Paul was not relying on himself when he said he was able to do all things; he was relying on Jesus Christ, for he said he could do all things "through Christ."

Consider again the wide sweep of the Book of Philippians, as revealed in the key verses. The focus of attention of each chapter is on Jesus Christ. Throughout this letter we have been presented with "Christ our life" (1:21), "Christ our mind" (2:5), "Christ our goal" (3:10) and "Christ our strength" (4:13).

The supreme message for us to grasp from Paul's letter to the Philippians is that we should be wholly and absolutely mastered by Christ. We should be captives of the Lord. He is the one and only resource of power we need.

Even as Solomon asked for wisdom and understanding to judge God's people and was granted it (see I Kings 3:9-12), so we need to seek first the kingdom of God and His righteousness, and God will provide us with all we need (see Matt. 6:33). It is important, however, that we seek with the right motives. If we seek spiritual things only to elevate ourselves in the eyes of others, God will not grant them to us. But if we seek to know God better and to honor Him in daily living, He will meet our individual needs.

Concerning the word "do" in Philippians 4:13, there is no Greek word in the verse that is the basis for this word. It is literally, "I am strengthened," or "I am enabled." Paul was able to bear all things, to do all things and to dare all things "through Christ."

Verse 13 should be taken in context with verses 11 and 12, in which Paul enumerated all he had learned and had been instructed in. In a specific sense, verse 13 refers to adjusting to circumstances, and Paul had learned he could adjust to any circumstance because of Christ's enabling power. Paul's efforts did not give him the ability to adjust—Christ strengthened him. Because of his relationship to Christ and his confidence in Him, Paul was equal to anything.

The word "through" in the expression "through Christ" (v. 13, KJV) is really the word "in," which expresses our oneness with Christ. The fact that we are united to Christ is seen in such verses as John 15:5: "He who abides in Me, and I in him, he bears much fruit; for apart from Me you can do nothing."

Philippians 4:13 climaxes all we have studied in Philippians. It is important to realize it is not just Christ giving us strength; Christ *is* our strength. Ephesians 6:10 says, "Be strong in the Lord, and in the strength of His might."

The word "strengtheneth" (Phil. 4:13, KJV) is in the Greek present tense, which emphasizes continuous action. Paul was stressing that Christ was continually strengthening him. Christ constantly replenishes our strength and enables us to do anything that is His will. This continuous strengthening is a moment-by-moment, hour-by-hour and day-by-day experience for the believer.

Someone has said, "How often do we attempt work for God to the limit of our incompetency rather than to the limit of God's omnipotency?"

As we depend on our all-powerful God, He will enable us to do anything necessary. So we should not pray, "God, give me strength." We should pray, "God, I accept You as my strength." We can make such a distinction only as we realize that Christ indwells us for the purpose of strengthening, or enabling, us.

The Believer's Responsibility

In Philippians 4:13, Paul did not say that Christ did everything and he did nothing. Paul did not have a let-go-and-let-God approach to Christian living. Rather, his emphasis was on the ability of the believer to do everything through Christ.

The cooperation of the believer with the work of Christ is seen in Philippians 2:12,13: "Work out your own salvation with fear and trembling. For it is God which worketh in you both to will and to do of his good pleasure" (KJV). The believer has to cooperate with God or else what has been accomplished by God within him will not be expressed through his life. We should come to the Lord and say, "I am at Your disposal. You can use my body—mouth, hands, eyes, lips, ears—just the way You want to use them."

The relationship of individual responsibility to the work of God is also seen in John 7:37,38: "Jesus stood and cried out, saying, 'If any man is thirsty, let him come to Me and drink. He who believes in Me, as the Scripture said, "From his innermost being shall flow rivers of living water." ' " Notice the individual responsibility—the person must be thirsty and must come to Christ. So the person who desires to have the power of God expressed in his life and who then puts himself at God's disposal will experience Christ's strengthening for anything he needs. Just as one drinks a glass of water, so we need to accept what God provides for us. When we come to Christ and in faith believe Him (appropriate His strength) to accomplish what He has promised, we will discover the truth of what He said in John 7:38. Verse 39 reveals that Christ's statement was a reference to the Holy Spirit. The indwelling Spirit makes all this possible as we desire the things of God and come to Christ by faith to have them worked out in our lives.

We must remember, however, that God requires the cooperation of the individual believer before He will do a work in his life. God enhances the new, regenerated personality, but He does not supplant it. That is an important distinction because some Christians seem to believe that God does not use the human personality at all. However, God never ignores the personality He has given us; He uses it and empowers our abilities rather than setting them aside.

Moses is an example of the way God used an individual in accomplishing His will. The Book of Exodus reveals that for 40 years Moses was trained in the house of Pharaoh. When Moses realized that God wanted him to lead the Israelites out of Egypt, he presented himself with all the prestige and knowledge he had, but the people refused to accept his leadership. During the next 40 years in the desert, God taught Moses many valuable lessons. God brought Moses so low that Moses came to a complete end of himself. At that time— and only at that time—the Lord told Moses, "Now you shall see what I will do to Pharaoh" (6:1). Moses was not simply going to be an onlooker; God used Moses in accomplishing

His will. Moses' total personality was involved, but Moses had learned to rely on the Lord instead of on himself.

In considering that Philippians 4:13 reveals the believer's ability to do anything because of the indwelling Christ, think of the possibilities this has as it relates to what we have already studied. It shows the possibility of standing fast (v. 1), the possibility of living in moderation (v. 5), the possibility of having a carefree life (vv. 6,7), the possibility of controlling one's thought life (v. 8), the possibility of living a contented life (vv. 11,12) and the possibility of living a fully strengthened life (v. 13).

The secret to all of this lies in Christ. This is why Paul said, "Christ in you, the hope of glory" (Col. 1:27, KJV). Paul's recognition of Christ's work in him is expressed in Colossians 1:29: "Which mightily works within me." We will witness the power of Christ as we recognize His presence in us.

It is imperative to remember four key words: "I can . . . through Christ" (Phil. 4:13, KJV). A believer should never use only the first two words because we are only "self-sufficient in Christ's sufficiency" (Amplified).

Knowing this, each believer is faced with the question, What am I going to do about it? It is so easy to learn some spiritual truth and to think that it is all right for others but that it will not work for me. As someone has said, "So what I can do I ought to do, and what I ought to do I will do, and what I will do I am able to do—in Christ Jesus."

Worshipful Giving

As Paul wrote to the believers in Philippi, he acknowledged the gift they had sent him. However, he wanted to make it clear that he was not really dependent on their gifts because he could live in any state that God intended for him. Philippians 4:14-16 continues Paul's remarks concerning their gift: "Notwithstanding ye have well done, that ye did communicate with my affliction. Now ye Philippians know also, that in the beginning of the gospel, when I departed from Macedonia, no church communicated with me as concerning giving and receiving, but ye only. For even in Thessalonica ye sent once and again unto my necessity" (KJV).

Reward for the Giver

Paul was grateful for the gift of the Philippians, not because he was anxious for, or desired, gifts but because he knew God was keeping the books and that due credit would be given to the giver. This is evident from Philippians 4:17: "Not because I desire a gift: but I desire fruit that may abound to your account" (KJV).

Paul was not ungrateful for their gift. Even though he could have remained content without it, he accepted it and was grateful for it. But he was especially glad for it because he knew due credit would be given by God to those responsible.

We must not forget that God is the one keeping the books. Someday each believer will stand before God to be rewarded or to have rewards withheld, depending on his faithfulness. Paul said, "For we must all appear before the judgment seat of Christ, that each one may be recompensed for his deeds in the body, according to what he has done, whether good or bad" (II Cor. 5:10). This verse can either scare us or thrill us, depending on our faithfulness to the Lord. Whatever we have done—good or bad—is recorded in the books of heaven, even though no one else may know about it.

Jesus said, "Behold, I am coming quickly, and My reward is with Me, to render to every man according to what he has done" (Rev. 22:12). Faithfulness to the Lord will not go unrewarded.

Concerning our motives in spiritual matters, Jesus said, "Beware of practicing your righteousness before men to be noticed by them; otherwise you have no reward with your Father who is in heaven. When therefore you give alms, do not sound a trumpet before you, as the hypocrites do in the synagogues and in the streets, that they may be honored by men. Truly I say to you, they have their reward in full. But when you give alms, do not let your left hand know what your right hand is doing that your alms may be in secret; and your Father who sees in secret will repay you" (Matt. 6:1-4).

Let us not be concerned about publicizing what we do for the Lord. If we do, we already have our reward because we did it for self-glory. When our motivation is to glorify the

Lord, we will not be concerned about publicizing what we do. And in that case, the Lord will reward us fully.

What a difference it makes when we remember that God is keeping the books. Whenever I think of this truth, I am reminded of John Paton, who worked closely with me for several years but who is now with the Lord. Brother Paton's responsibility was editing and rewriting my messages for publication. One time I asked him, "John, how can you take it? I get all the credit for the fine work you are doing behind the scenes." Smiling, he pointed to heaven and said, "I know who keeps the books." What a gracious attitude he had, and what a fine job he did because he knew he was really serving the Lord.

Paul was especially pleased for the gift from the Philippians because he knew God was keeping the books, and the gift was fruit that would abound to their account. Think of it. By giving to Paul, their own account before the Lord was increased! As a savings account receives compounded interest on the money deposited, so the believer's account increases before the Lord as he gives to others. This is a reminder of what Jesus will say when He returns to earth and rewards those who have treated the Jews well: "Truly I say to you, to the extent that you did it to one of these brothers of Mine, even the least of them, you did it to Me" (25:40). This is one of God's principles—as we do well toward His own, we are rewarded.

God's Supplying of Needs

In concluding his letter to the Philippians, Paul stated what has become one of the favorite verses of many Christians: "But my God shall supply all your need according to his riches in glory by Christ Jesus" (4:19). Not only has this been a favorite verse to many believers, but some have also taken it as a life verse, endeavoring to build their lives around the principles stated in it. Regrettably, however, many misunderstand what Paul was communicating in this verse. As a result, they claim this great promise more by presumption than by true faith. Faith must be based on fact, or truth. What is the truth of this verse? Let us consider it carefully.

Verse 19 begins with the word "but." The Greek word itself
can mean not only "but" but also "and" or "moreover." The
verse is obviously connected with the preceding verses, especially verses 14-18. Verse 19 cannot be understood apart
from these preceding verses. Some Christians have claimed
verse 19 but have not met the conditions of the preceding
verses; therefore, they are unwarranted in expecting God to
keep His promise of verse 19. And when they see that God
has not fulfilled what they consider to be a promise, it can
make their lives a shipwreck. Thus, it is very important to
understand the context of verse 19.

We will never realize the tremendous provision of verse 19
until we have met its spiritual and circumstantial requirements. Almost every promise in the Bible has one or more
conditions which must be met before God's promise is
fulfilled.

Philippians 4:19 says, "God shall supply all your need"
(KJV). We see, then, that there must be a need before God will
supply. We must not presume on this promise and run ahead
of God with plans of our own. Neither should we presume on
God for all our wants or be careless in spending God's
money. God does not promise to supply all of our wants, only
our needs. The slothful, the spendthrift or the selfish person
cannot claim the promise of Philippians 4:19. There must be
a legitimate need. Those who are slothful and unwilling to
work or who are over-ambitious to gain things need not
expect to have this verse fulfilled in their lives.

It should also be understood that God meets our need for a
purpose—not to relieve us of our responsibility but because
He has given us responsibility. When God gives us a responsibility to fulfill, we can count on His supplying all of the
needs that are necessary to accomplish it.

It was God's will that the believers in Philippi be responsible for helping to take care of Paul's needs. Because they
were faithful in exercising that responsibility, Paul assured
them that God would supply their needs.

As Paul wrote to the believers in Corinth to encourage
them to give toward the needs of other saints, he said, "He
who sows sparingly shall also reap sparingly; and he who
sows bountifully shall also reap bountifully" (II Cor. 9:6).
This is another principle of God and implies a condition—

before a person can reap bountifully, he must sow bountifully. Concerning giving, Paul also told the Corinthians, "Let each one do just as he has purposed in his heart; not grudgingly or under compulsion; for God loves a cheerful giver" (v. 7). What an important verse for us to keep in mind! For the Corinthians to fulfill their responsibility to give bountifully, Paul said, "God is able to make all grace abound toward you; that ye, always having all sufficiency in all things, may abound to every good work" (v. 8, KJV).

God's principle concerning giving is clearly stated in Luke 6:38: "Give, and it will be given to you; good measure, pressed down, shaken together, running over, they will pour into your lap. For whatever measure you deal out to others, it will be dealt to you in return."

Giving involves more than dollars and cents—it includes motives and attitudes. Some Christians tithe only because they think that God will bountifully reward them if they do. Such a motive is wrong because it is an attitude of giving in order to get.

The gift of the Philippians to Paul was an example of proper Christian giving. They gave not to get anything in return but because they loved Paul, who was serving the Lord they loved. Because of this, the Apostle Paul promised they would have their needs met by God.

Paul said, "My God" (Phil. 4:19, KJV). It is evident that to Paul, God was more than a distant provider. Paul knew God as One who "is at hand" (v. 5, KJV). Notice that he did not say "may" but "shall." When the conditions are met, one can count on God to be faithful to His Word. When such is the case, the believer can say with the psalmist, "The Lord is my shepherd; I shall not want" (Ps. 23:1, KJV).

In Philippians 4:19, Paul further added, "all your need" (KJV). No restrictions! Where there is a need, there is God's supply. Neither is there a restriction on the kinds of needs— spiritual, mental, financial, emotional, physical—all are included.

Philippians 4:19 also includes the significant phrase "according to his riches in glory" (KJV). Notice it does not say "out of " or "from" but "according to." There is a tremendous difference.

Suppose you need $10,000, so you present your request to a

millionaire, and he responds by giving you a ten-dollar bill. He has given to you out of his riches, or from his riches, but he has not given according to his riches. However, if he responds to your need by handing you his checkbook to fill in the amount, he has given according to his riches.

Philippians 4:19 refers to a fulfillment of God's promise, which is accomplished by His ability because of His abundance. No one can estimate the resources of God; His wealth is beyond computing. When we have met the conditions, God has promised to supply our need. And no need is too great for Him to meet because of His riches in glory.

God's riches are all ours "by Christ Jesus" (v. 19, KJV). Ephesians 1:3 reveals that God "has blessed us with every spiritual blessing in the heavenly places in Christ." Although these riches are ours because of our position in Christ, we must appropriate them for ourselves, even as Joshua actually had to take the land which God had given to him. God told Joshua, "Every place on which the sole of your foot treads, I have given it to you, just as I spoke to Moses" (Josh. 1:3). The land belonged to Joshua positionally, but he actually had to appropriate it step by step in order for it to be his personally.

Doxology

Philippians 4:20 is a triumphant note which summarizes Paul's response to what he had said in all four chapters of his letter to the Philippians: "Now unto God and our Father be glory for ever and ever. Amen" (KJV). By the time Paul had reached this point, he realized all that needed to be added was a doxology! The Amplified Bible renders this verse: "To our God and Father be glory forever and ever—through the endless eternities of the eternities. Amen, so be it."

Having given this benediction because of the goodness of God, Paul drew to a close his letter to the Philippians. The remaining verses contain exchanges of greetings and a complementary close to his letter. Paul wrote: "Salute every saint in Christ Jesus. The brethren which are with me greet you. All the saints salute you, chiefly they that are of Caesar's household" (vv. 21,22, KJV).

Paul's reference to Caesar's household is an indication

that he was writing to the Philippians from Rome, the imperial headquarters. Under normal circumstances, Paul probably would never have been allowed to contact anyone connected with the imperial establishment. But in the outworking of the sovereignty of God, circumstances had brought Paul to the capital of the great Roman Empire where he won converts for Christ among those associated with the Emperor. From these important contacts for Christ the gospel would be spread throughout the Roman Empire as those of Caesar's household shared their faith in Christ with those who had business in the Roman capital.

After exchanging greetings, Paul climaxed his letter by referring to the grace of God: "The grace of our Lord Jesus Christ be with you all. Amen" (v. 23, KJV). Paul concluded his letter much the same as he began it, with the word "grace." The word "grace" was more than a salutation (1:2) and a complementary close (4:23) of a letter. This one word reminded Paul that he deserved eternal condemnation but that God had sent His only Son to pay the penalty for his sin. Paul had trusted in Christ as his personal Saviour and had received forgiveness of sin and eternal life.

This marvelous grace of God motivated Paul to do all he did in taking the gospel to a confused, Christ-hating world. Paul's service of love had brought him much suffering, but God had worked through him to accomplish many victories, such as the salvation of the Philippians and those of Caesar's household.

The same grace of God is available to each person today. And like Paul, anyone who places his trust in Christ as his personal Saviour from sin receives forgiveness of sin and eternal life. Salvation involves a transfer of trust—from oneself and what he can do to Jesus Christ and what He has done for him.

Have you trusted Christ as your personal Saviour? If not, do so before it is eternally too late. Then you will be able to apply Paul's words to yourself: "The grace of our Lord Jesus Christ be with you all. Amen" (v. 23, KJV).